I0462761

FLORENT DEFONTIS

How Analytics Can Help You Drive Growth and Beat the Competition

Master Analytics for Business Growth: A Complete Guide

Contents

1

A BRIEF WORD ABOUT ME AND WHY I WROTE THIS BOOK

Analytics is ever-changing. It changes so quickly that, at times, I feel as though I am still learning – a student of data that is always absorbing new ideas and new opportunities for better data collection and analysis.

When I first started writing this book, I paused. There are already hundreds of books both online and offline about app analytics, and I had a variety of questions:

- What makes me an expert?
- What can I say that other experts haven't?
- What value can I bring to the reader, who may or may not have an analytics background?

The truth is, not long ago, I didn't feel analytics was that helpful. I was – and am – a software engineer, and analytics felt like a hurdle that I had to cross to do my job effectively.

But after toying around with a few analytic tools of my own a few years ago, I found that the problem wasn't the tools. The problem was me.

Although to be honest, it was also the tools.

Essentially, what I realized was that I was coming into the world of analytics as a novice, trying to build a home without ever taking a single class. That meant I was faced with this daunting task and no idea of how to complete it.

But I was also using these low-quality tools.

Analytic tools are far too often flash over substance. No amount of training can prepare me to build a home using only a toothpick as a tool, and I was coming into each project with no idea of how to start in the first place. That's why analytics always seemed like an unnecessary burden.

In 2016, the sales of one of the mobile applications we developed for a client started to decline. It took us 4 days to troubleshoot, only to find that the only issue was a Purchase button that no longer worked after an iPhone iOS update. A simple fix.

There were 2 different analytics tools installed on this app, and neither of them was able to spot this obvious error. It was then I realized that, while I may not have been the best user, the analytics tools themselves were failing to adapt to the needs of the market.

In a world that increasingly depends on automation and artificial intelligence, something was wrong. It was then I dived deeper into the world of analytics, and it was my experience that brought me here, both with my company and with you.

I hope you'll find this eBook helpful and if you have any question or feedback, please get in touch at flo@air360.io

2

INTRODUCTION - WHAT IS GROWTH?

What is Growth?

Growth is a multi-dimensional construct. It depends (mostly) on your business goals as to how and when you'll consider *growth* to be enough.

Generally, *growth* is defined as:

"A business that is generating positive cash flows. A business that increases its earnings at a faster pace than the economy's pace."

So growth is all about how well your business is doing as compared to all the other businesses in the same industry (or other industries).

Your business grows when you have the right resources, data, and research. When you make the right decisions at those critical moments. It grows when you know what you have to do and why you have to do it.

Data plays a significant role in decision-making and thus

growth. For instance, if data shows that customers like Feature A more than Feature B, you can offer Feature A without a second thought to your app. You know it will work.

In the absence of data, you'll have to create and test multiple features to figure out what your customers like. This testing and tweaking can take months or maybe years. Don't forget the resources you'll spend on this testing process.

Having data isn't enough rather how you analyze the available data is essential.

Data analysis or analytics is essential for growth. It takes the guesswork out from the equation. You know what exactly you have to do.

Because data don't lie.

One of the core purposes of analytics in the app market is to help you grow your app and company.

You need data for decision-making for all the customer lifecycle stages. This means you have to implement growth across all the AARRR framework for your app.

You need powerful data and analytics to ensure growth across all these stages for your business. Here is an overview of what these stages are all about.

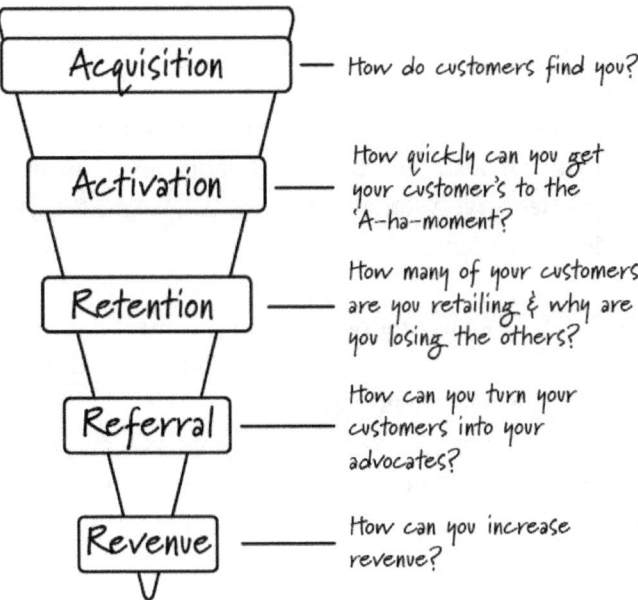

Dave McClure's Pirate Metrics For Startup Growth

Acquisition — How do customers find you?

Activation — How quickly can you get your customer's to the 'A-ha-moment?'

Retention — How many of your customers are you retailing & why are you losing the others?

Referral — How can you turn your customers into your advocates?

Revenue — How can you increase revenue?

Acquisition

This is the stage where you acquire new customers for your business. The idea is to reach more people so that you can acquire customers for your business.

More customers at this stage mean you'll have more customers pushed down to the other stages of the funnel.

Using growth techniques to bring more people to your websites via PPC ads, search ads, search engines, and other sources is the best you can do.

Activation

It is a customer lifecycle stage that's mostly used by SaaS companies though it isn't necessary. Activation is the customer's first experience with your product. You need to make this first experience awesome.

How?

By critically analyzing how customers interact with your product, what features they use, what is the first thing they do after using your product, etc.

If you have an app, it gets easier to analyze user behavior and actions they take after downloading your app. Monitoring user behavior will reveal a wealth of data on what to optimize and how to make the first experience awesome.

Retention

Are you retaining customers? What's the difference between customers you retain and customers you lose after the acquisition stage?

If you lose more customers after the first experience (acquisition), you need to improve the acquisition stage. If you retain more customers, that's a great job – improve it.

If customer acquisition rate is higher than the churn rate, your business is growing (*Growth*). This should be your target.

This is where analytics plays its role. Collect data on every customer interaction. Generate reports. Analyze behavior. Collect feedback. Understand what is making customers churn.

That's the perfect approach to growth.

Referral

This is a crucial step for growth. You need to convert your existing customers into brand advocates. Persuade them to bring more people.

Here is the thing: If a customer is happy with your product, support, and business, he/she will refer your product to others.

But you need to incentivize your customers so they refer your app to their friends. That's how you can grow your business exponentially without doing a lot of hard work.

Dropbox grew by 3900% with its referral program. It doubled its user base every 3 months all with its referral program.

Interesting, right?

Revenue

Finally, it's all about revenue. If you managed to do well with the previous four stages, getting revenue won't be an issue. Dropbox increased its valuation to a ten billion dollar company primarily because of its referral program and heaps of users.

When you have loyal customers who are referring your product to their friends, generating revenue gets a whole lot easier. At this stage, you need to figure out how you can increase revenue from existing customers (revenue per customer). That is, increasing customer lifetime value (CLV).

You need data on how to do it effectively.

At the end of the day, growth is all about how you collect and analyze data.

How Does Analytics Make Growth Better?

Growth is driven by analytics, I'm sure you now know it.

Analytics provide you deep insights on what to improve, how to improve it, what are your business strengths and weaknesses, and how to overcome them.

Analytics provide you with actionable and data-driven answers to all of the following (and many other) questions:

- Who are your ideal customers?
- How your customers find your product?
- What value does your product offer to its users?
- What marketing techniques are most effective?
- How users engage with your app?
- When and why users leave your app?

These are only a few of the many questions that analytics will answer.

Based on these answers, you can create a growth model that can be used to boost engagement, increase conversions, increase revenue, and grow your business exponentially.

How to do it?

This is what exactly you'll find in this book.

Hold your questions and keep reading. By the time you'll finish reading this book, you'll have all your queries answered and you'll be able to use analytics to grow your business like a pro.

CHAPTER #1: EVERYTHING YOU NEED TO KNOW ABOUT ANALYTICS

If you watch *The Fast and The Furious* on Netflix, you'll get a Vin Diesel movie in your personal recommendation the next day. And if you spend a few good months with Netflix, you'll notice that they show you recommendations that perfectly match your taste which you can't ignore.

That's the power of analytics.

It's not just Netflix but all the businesses big and small use data to better understand their customers and to grow their business.

Analytics and data are the two buzzwords that you get to read everywhere. The way how data is generated and analyzed has changed a lot recently. In fact, it has changed enormously in a decade or so. Think of big data and IoT that have transformed the way how you collect and analyze data.

In order to fully understand the basics of analytics, it is essential to know data inside out. This chapter covers everything on analytics and how it can change the fate of your business.

What is Analytics?

Analytics is *the conversion of data into meaningful insights that can be used for decision-making and can be applied to your business.* If this wasn't easy enough, here is an easier definition: *Analyzing the data and using it to grow your business.*

Techopedia defines it as:

"The scientific process of discovering and communicating the meaningful patterns which can be found in data."

Florian Zettelmeyer, who is a professor of marketing in Kellogg School of Management at Northwestern University, says:

"You don't have to be a data scientist rather you just have to have the basic understanding of how analytics work and how (and where) it can add value to your business."

When you remove or tweak a landing page with a poor conversion rate, you have used analytics to decide which landing page needs to go. Similarly, when you switch to how-to articles on your blog because they outperform other types of article formats, you do so based on data.

All businesses use some sort of analytics on a daily basis implicitly or explicitly.

Data and Analytics

Analytics relies on data. In order to use analytics for growth, you need to have data – a lot of it.

Analytics is driven by data so if you don't have meaningful data, analytics isn't for you. The first step towards analytics is to collect data.

Where to collect data?

Collect data about everything and when I say everything I literally mean everything. The more data you have, the better. Collect data about customers, buying patterns, conduct surveys and interviews, and get data from third-parties to better understand your target audience, customers, and internal customers.

Having data isn't enough, you need to have appropriate tools to clean, organize, and analyze it. When you have a lot of data, it should be handled smartly. If not used right, you won't be able to make sense of it.

Analytics vs. Analysis

A lot of businesses use these two terms interchangeably. While both analytics and analysis are closely related in several aspects but these are two different terms.

The analysis is focused on what has already happened (*the past*) while analytics is focused on what will happen (*the future*). This is the reason why you can use analytics for business growth while you can't use analysis to predict growth.

The analysis is used to show what has happened and is used to represent past perform to stakeholders. For instance, you can generate reports on how your business performed in the last 12 months and show it to the board of directors and CEO.

Analytics isn't used to assess past performance rather it is used to predict future based on what has already happened. It is used for decision-making and inference.

Here is a detailed comparison between data analysis and analytics by Educba:

Analytics here is all about using it to predict the future and take appropriate decisions that will lead to growth and sales.

Analytics Statistics

The following stats on analytics will show you how important it is for your business and how it can help you push your business in the right direction:

1. Businesses that use insights from data analytics see 30% more growth per year and these businesses are expected to take as much as $1.8 trillion annually by 2021. (Forrester)
2. Data-driven organizations are 23x more likely to acquire new customers, 6x more likely to retain them, and 19x more likely to be more profitable than their counterparts. (McKinsey)
3. 90% of businesses say that data and analytics are the keys to digital transformation in their organizations. (MicroStrategy)
4. Businesses that use big data for decision-making increased their profits by 8% and reduced costs by 10%. (BARC)
5. 36.6% of businesses use analytics to drive customer acquisition. (HBR)
6. Businesses that don't use analytics for sales and marketing decisions miss up to 20% increase in ROI. (Forbes)
7. Only 25% of businesses collect customer data for analytics. (Forbes)
8. Businesses that don't collect and maintain important customer data see 34% lower conversion rate as compared to their counterparts. (AccuData)
9. 90% of the world's data was created between 2015 and 2016 alone. (IBM)
10. 95% of businesses have to manage some kind of unstructured data. (Forbes)

11. 95% of all data generated by 2025 will be by the Internet of Things. (Data Age)
12. Only 7% of businesses and marketers are able to effectively deliver real-time data-driven marketing engagements across multiple touchpoints. (CMO Council)

Isn't it enough to make you realize the importance of data and analytics?

Types of Analytics

There are different types of data analytics. In other words, there are different ways to make use of the data that you have. The four approaches to data analytics include:

1. Prescriptive
2. Predictive
3. Diagnostic
4. Descriptive

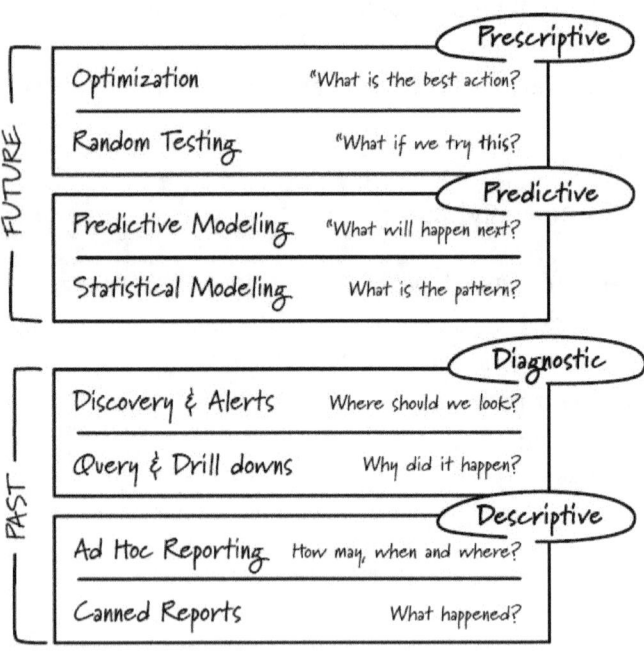

The Four Types of Data Analytics

FUTURE

Optimization	"What is the best action?
Random Testing	"What if we try this?

Prescriptive

Predictive Modeling	"What will happen next?
Statistical Modeling	What is the pattern?

Predictive

PAST

Discovery & Alerts	Where should we look?
Query & Drill downs	Why did it happen?

Diagnostic

Ad Hoc Reporting	How may, when and where?
Canned Reports	What happened?

Descriptive

1. Prescriptive Analytics

This is the most common type of data analytics which is primarily used for optimization. The data is used to answer the best possible action that will lead to better results.

The idea is to use data analytics for the *prescription*. For instance, Google Maps tells you an alternate route when a route has excessive traffic. This is based on data that Google Maps collects.

Similarly, when you publish a new landing page to test things out, you're actually involved in prescriptive analytics. Whenever you're trying new things to get answers, you're doing prescriptive analytics.

2. Predictive Analytics

Predictive analytics is used for forecasting and predicting the future. This is the type of analytics that you have to master if you're interested in using analytics for growth.

It is used to identify patterns that help you figure out what will happen next. Predictive analytics finds trends by hypotheses testing, defining the relationship between variables, finding correlations, and inspecting causality.

For instance, when you use A/B testing to see what landing page performs better in terms of conversion rate, you're involved in predictive analytics where you create and test hypotheses.

3. Diagnostic Analytics

It is related to the past and is used to answer questions like why something happened in the first place. The idea is to diagnose the reasons that led to a certain situation.

For instance, sales of a certain product decreased in the target market. You'll dig deep to find why it happened so it can be avoided. This type of analytics helps you diagnose and fix issues which leads to damage reduction.

Once you know why something happened, you can take precautionary measures. It isn't always about something bad rather diagnostic analytics is very handy when it comes to identifying healthy stuff. For instance, a surge in conversion for a squeeze page needs to be further analyzed using diagnostic analytics so you can do it again.

4. Descriptive Analytics

Descriptive analytics is the basic analytics type that is used to figure out what happened, why it happened, how it happened, etc. It is used to describe what has happened in the past.

The best example of descriptive analytics are reports that are presented to management and stakeholders. For instance, monthly sales, revenue, number of the new customers acquired, etc. These are all types of descriptive analytics that form the basis of analytics in your business.

So what type of analytics you need to use?

Use all types of analytics.

While your focus should be on future (and prediction), therefore, you should devote the most time to predictive and prescriptive analytics but you shouldn't ignore diagnostic and descriptive analytics as these guide you on what you did in the past that worked and didn't work.

Analytics in any form is useful.

Analytics Benefits

Analytics offers your business with a lot of benefits and these benefits are the reason why I have to write a book on analytics. Unfortunately, businesses and marketers don't fully understand the importance and benefits of analytics that they can derive.

If you don't know how powerful and beneficial analytics can be for your business and its growth, you'll always hesitate to invest in analytics. You won't be able to allocate appropriate resources to analytics.

It is, therefore, essential to understand how analytics will benefit your business and how it will help with growth.

1. Prediction

If there is one thing that you can't ignore about data analytics, its predictability. This is the number one reason you should use analytics for business growth. In fact, the whole point is to use analytics to predict future and move in the right direction by taking the right decisions.

Analytics will tell you exactly what you should do, how to do it, and what to expect. The predictions aren't always 100% accurate but mostly are, because these predictions aren't mere propositions rather these are based on data and numbers.

And numbers don't lie.

The best-known example of how you can use analytics for prediction is credit scoring. The credit score is entirely based on predictive analytics where customer data is collected from multiple sources (e.g. credit history, loans, credit cards, bill payments, etc.) and the individual is ranked accordingly.

Another example of how analytics can help with prediction is CRM tools that collect data continuously and recommend appropriate products that a customer is more likely to purchase based on one's buying history.

Prediction across all levels throughout your business will eventually lead to growth and profitability.

2. Decision-Making

Making the right decisions is tough especially in today's fast-paced economy. You have to have data at your fingertips to make the right decisions. This is where analytics become must-have for any business that wants to stay on the top.

You have to make several decisions on any given day ranging from what marketing techniques to use to product extensions to customer support channels to delivery options to the shipping cost and more. Your decisions can be arbitrary or you can use data to guide your decision-making process.

Arbitrary decision-making often fails so it is the last thing that you should do. Data, on the other hand, shows you the real picture, sets the right expectations, and shows you how things will be if you choose a specific path.

Everything becomes clear when decision-making is powered by analytics.

3. Customer Experience

Great customer experience doesn't just win customers but it plays a significant role in your company's growth. Statistics show that moderate improvement in customer experience will increase the revenue of a $1 billion company by $775 million over three years.

It is expected that customer experience will be more important than product and price by 2020. A Gartner report claims that more than 80% of businesses will compete mainly on the basis of customer experience in the future.

Isn't it more than enough?

Customer experience is driven by nothing else than analytics. The better you know your customers, your audience, their interests, their preferences, etc., the better it is. A clear understanding of who your customers are and what are their core needs and problems can only be accessed with data.

It doesn't matter how you collect all the information about your customers, the thing that really matters is how you use it to provide them with a superior customer experience that will eventually lead to sustainable growth.

But yes, data collection and analytics are the first two steps to customer experience success. I have to admit that improvement in customer experience is one of the best benefits that you get with analytics because you get to know your customers better. You can fully understand them, their needs, and what type of experience they prefer.

4. Optimization

Optimization is related to customer experience but it isn't always about customer experience. Optimization or Conversion Rate Optimization (CRO) is a much broader term that covers pretty much everything related to your business, especially marketing.

The purpose of optimization is to make your website user-friendly and to improve conversions. This is something that you can't do without analytics. Think of A/B test and hypotheses testing, this is all done to optimize the website, marketing campaigns, products, and more. And that's where data plays a significant role.

When you have to test two different offers, two or more landing pages, homepage, CTAs, newsletters, social media posts, content types, etc. you need data to help you choose the best possible alternative. That's what makes analytics relevant as well as important for optimization across all levels and channels throughout your organization.

5. Competitive Advantage

Analytics gives your business a competitive edge over your competitors. When you collect and analyze data for decision-making, and your competitors don't do it at all or if you do it better than your competitors, you'll eventually kill the competition.

Think of Google, Facebook, and Amazon, why it's hard for new entrants to beat these giants? Because they have mastered analytics and they have heaps and heaps of data that it's impossible to create a better ad network than Google AdWords or to offer better targeting than Facebook Ads.

If it wasn't about data, creating a social networking site like Facebook isn't a big deal. A team of coders can create a better Facebook alternative but it won't have the data that Facebook has collected over the years about its users.

Makes sense, right?

That's what analytics does to your business. When you constantly collect and analyze data about your business and customers, you transform yourself into an industry leader and gain a competitive advantage that's hard to imitate.

6. Profitability

This is obvious, of course. When everything is moving in the right direction for any business, generating profit doesn't seem to be a challenge.

But there is more...

You can use analytics to increase profitability specifically. You can set realistic revenue and sales objectives by looking at the data, you can offer better products that your customer will buy, you can identify areas where you're wasting money without any result, and so on.

There are so many ways you can use analytics to increase revenue and take your business to the next level. There is a lot that you can get from analytics. When you start seeing results, you get to make sense of everything that's related to your business. It just gets better and better.

Long-Term Benefits of Analytics

Analytics has several long-term benefits that your business can enjoy.

Big companies like Google, Facebook, and Amazon have one thing in common – data. These major corporate giants are data-centered companies that collect heaps of data about every customer interaction. This data drives their decision-making.

According to research, businesses that use detailed customer behavior data that is capable of delivering real change within the organization outperform their counterparts by 85% in sales growth and more than 25% in gross margin.

Data really matters.

Data is mandatory for success.

If you're not using analytics, chances are one of your competitors will use it either now or later. If you're not using all of the behavioral data you have collected in some form, the ones that are will take advantage of any opportunity and steal potential conversions from your funnel.

The story doesn't end here. I'm sure you know the data-side of analytics but there is more. The benefits go beyond simply making better decisions. Here are some of the major long-term benefits of using and incorporating analytics throughout your business:

Analytics Gives Purpose

Employees who understand that decisions are made through data know what they're doing is valuable. It gives them an idea of why they're doing what they're supposed to do.

It also helps your entire team understand how and why to work together to achieve a common goal.

Analytics Gives Performance

Once they've made those changes, analytics shows your entire team the effect of their work. If properly enacted, the improvement in conversions provides positive feedback that shows that their performance was worthwhile.

Analytics Gives Motivation

The positive feedback motivates your employees. Your team exerts more effort next time around. They push themselves hard. Thus, analytics may mean that your entire organization performs better than competing companies.

Not only does analytics give you actionable information that will grow your business – it also helps your company operate efficiently, giving you the psychological tools as well as the data-driven decisions that will help you succeed.

You don't need to be a tech giant to use analytics. You just need to be willing and should have the right tools to move forward with your analysis.

It is as simple as that.

Analytics Mistakes and How to Avoid Them

It's not necessarily difficult to understand why analytics could – or should – be valuable.

But if you ask the majority of business owners if they have benefitted from their analytics, many of them will say "No" and even more of them will say that what they learned was valuable, but not earth-shattering.

In my experience, the number one reason is that a fairly large number of businesses are doing analytics wrong. They make preventable mistakes that affect their ability to benefit from the data.

What kind of mistakes they make? Here is an overview.

Mistake #1: Not Using Right Analytics Tools

Tools like Google Analytics can have their uses but "enterprise-class" tools are probably not identifying all of the data that is important to you. What this means is that you might be using a wrong analytics tool.

Not all analytics tools are equally good and useful.

You need to collect data across all the customer lifecycle stages – not just data on website visits. Google Analytics, for instance, collects data for acquisition stage exceptionally well. But when it comes to the activation stage, it doesn't do a great job.

That's where you need access to the right analytics tool.

When you don't have a tool for data collection, your valuable data will be lost. Once lost, you NEVER get it back.

Mistake #2: Measuring Irrelevant Metrics

Data on metrics like page views or sessions can be fun. It is generally useless.

Here is why.

Any data that doesn't take into account critical metrics like user behavior or doesn't utilize other data within the system to maximize detail isn't worth assessing. It's just fun.

Are you making this mistake?

Mistake #3: Complicated = Good

Complication doesn't mean the analytics tool is great.

In fact, it can be the other way around.

If it takes a MENSA-level genius to understand how to use the tool then it is a bad tool and one that is likely to lead to further errors.

Make Analytics Mistake-Free

Make your analytics free from these and other mistakes.

Businesses that keep the above mistakes in mind can instantly improve the value that these tools bring to the workplace. Because the more time you spend getting analytics wrong, the less time you have beating the competitors that are getting analytics right.

How to Find the Right Analytics Tool for Your Business

The most important step for gaining value from analytics is choosing the right tool.

With the right software, you don't need a genius to analyze data. You don't need a team to manage data and generate reports. It's a built-in feature. You just have to implement the tracking code and the tool will handle the rest.

Choosing the right software is often the most important step towards avoiding mistakes. If you do it right, you can save money and other resources.

But before you choose the best analytics tool, try to figure out what you're looking for in a tool. What type of tool do you need? What you intend to track and measure? What sales funnel stage you intend to track?

Choosing the right tool gets easier if you link it to a problem your business is facing. Here are a few actual problems that your business can solve with an appropriate analytics tool:

· What is the average output value (revenue) of repeat customers?

- What is the cost of new customers and how does that compare?
- What is the reason that buyers are abandoning their online shopping carts?
- How does marketing campaign X compare in both cost and ROI to marketing campaign Y?
- How do customers that used promotional codes affect revenue compared to those that did not?
- What effect, if any, does live chat support have on checkout rates?

You get the idea, right?

The right analytics tool helps you solve the problem that restricts growth.

The tool doesn't have to be complicated. It should be dead simple and will offer all of the following features (minimum):

- It should segment users. You can't do analytics without segmentation.
- It should track everything automatically. Almost all analytic tools do it automatically.
- The tool provides you with reports that are easy-to-understand. This is the crux. If you can't understand the report, you won't be able to use analytics for decision-making.

If your analytics tool has these three features (at least) and it will help you solve a growth-related problem your business is facing, go for it.

4

CHAPTER #2: HOW TO COLLECT DATA FOR ANALYTICS?

By now, you must have realized the importance of analytics and the massive role it plays in business growth. What's more important than analytics is data. You can't do analytics without data.

Its data that you have to make sense of using analytics.

There are several sources of data. Sometimes it has to be collected while at other occasions it is readily available. For instance, you'll need to conduct surveys to understand the interest, problems, and preferences of your ideal customers (target audience), you can't get this information without asking them.

On the other hand, how much an average customer spend in a lifetime with your brand is a piece of information that's already available. You don't have to collect this data.

Generally, you have to take steps to manage data so that it can be used for analytics. To get started, you need to collect data on several variables. You can't grow your business without market research and data collection.

There are several ways to collect data to power analytics. This chapter covers leading data collection techniques and methods.

1. Competitor Analysis

Tommy Hilfiger said:

"I looked at my competitors and I thought that, if they could do it, I could do it. And if, they are popular and doing well, I could compete with them."

So what exactly is competitor analysis? Here is a simple definition yet complete:

"Identifying your competitors and evaluating their strategies to determine their strengths and weaknesses relative to those of your own product or service."

Your competitors are your guide. They show you the path to success (or failure). If a competitor is doing something good, you need to replicate it. If a competitor has failed miserably at something, you need to figure out what went wrong and not to repeat the same mistakes.

This can't be done without analyzing your competitors. You need to collect data and use analytics to understand your competitors, their strategies, campaigns, and objectives.

Here are a few major benefits of competitor analysis:

1. Identify trends
2. Benchmarking
3. Identification of opportunities and threats
4. Idea generation
5. Product improvement
6. Customer experience improvement
7. Getting to know your competitors better

SWOT Analytics

Strengths:

- Same day Delivery within the city
- Urban core has 1 hour delivery
- High-quality foods
- 200+ Drivers
- Trusted and high exposure

Weaknesses:

- Costly
- No monthly subscription options Or scaled payment arrangement
- Inaccessible to a larger audience
- Poorly optimized SEO

Opportunities:

- Optimize current mobile app for responsiveness and built-in feedback
- Attract a larger wider target audience
- SEO focus can help drive a great amount of traffic and improve online rankings in a short span of time

Threats:

- Can operate at a loss to drive away competition
- Costly state laws to oversee grocery delivery and accountability under review

If you're interested in growing your business, you need to see what the industry leader is doing. You have to do better or at least do the same. In order to figure out what industry leader is doing, you need to spend heavily on research and analytics. You can't expect to get details about a market leader easily.

When you have the data, the next step is easy – you just have to replicate and improve.

The challenging task is competitor analysis.

And the big question is: *How to do competitor analysis to gather data to grow your own business?*

Competitor analysis is a step-by-step approach to identifying, categorizing, and examining your competitors. It is a three-step process:

1. Identify your competitors (and categorize them)
2. Competitor research
3. Compare your business and take action

Step #1: Identify Your Competitors

Seems quite obvious, right?

In most cases, it is. You know who your competitors are even before starting your business. Even if you know them all already, it is still recommended to revisit the list of your top competitors and consider updating it.

Use Google. Run search queries for keywords you're targeting and see who else is targeting them, what businesses are running ads for these terms, and who ranks at the top position in Google. Use multiple search terms and variants. Add all the competitors (both direct and indirect) to an Excel sheet.

The next step is categorizing your competitors. The best approach to categorization is to divide them into the following three categories:

1. Primary competitors (*Direct and lethal competitors*)
2. Secondary competitors (*Indirect competitors that are easy-to-deal with and aren't an as big threat as primary competitors*)

3. Tertiary competitors (*Friendly competitors that you can partner with at some stage*)

Primary competitors should be your main concern. You need to see what they're doing and how they're doing it. They pose a real threat to your business so make sure you put competitors in this category with extreme caution.

Step #2: Competitor Research

Here comes the real challenging task. Finding and categorizing your competitors isn't really a big deal, collecting information and analyzing them is.

The rule is simple: The more research you do, the better.

You need to find details about pricing strategy, sales funnel, offers, marketing strategy, marketing campaigns, content marketing, and more. You need to use a competitor spying tool such as SpyFu that gives you details about your competitors on PPC, SEO, keywords they're targeting, and more.

You can't find important competitor data without using tools. You have to use multiple tools to generate reports and find data that will eventually help you in analytics and decision-making.

Step #3: Compare and Improve

Finally, you need to compare your business with your competitors for all the data you have collected. How well you're doing, what else you can do to get better, and what are opportunities and threats that you have to look for.

SWOT analysis is your best bet. You need to list strengths, weaknesses, opportunities, and threats in an Excel sheet. Here is an example:

This will give you an idea of what exactly you can do and how to do it. The SWOT analysis will give you instant feedback on competitor analysis, however, the main purpose of this activity is to collect data.

Imagine, you have been collecting competitor data regularly

for the past 5 years. Think of information that you'll have about each competitor. You'll be able to predict their moves. This is the real beauty of analytics.

Not only will you be able to predict your competitor moves and strategies but you'll be able to take necessary steps to stay ahead of the competitors. This is all done by data and analytics.

2. Website Analysis

Your website is the biggest source of data that can power analytics across all levels. The website is how your ideal customers find you, interact with your brand, and connect with you. This means you can collect heaps of data from your website.

There are certain limitations that you have to face when you collect data from other sources (e.g. competitors) but you don't face any limitations when collecting data from your own website. You can get all the information you can using any tool you like.

Google Analytics, for instance, is a free analytics tool that provides you with the basic analysis of your website on metrics such as visitors, average time spent, location, device, etc. This will help you in finding answers to a lot of your queries.

If you need to analyze your website in great depth (which you should), you have to use other tools along with Google Analytics. Air360 provides you with additional information about your website and visitor behavior that you don't get with Google Analytics and other tools.

For instance, if you're interested in behavioral analytics, you can't do it with Google Analytics. That's something you can do with Air360. It provides you details on why visitors leave your website, what they do on a given page, where they click, how much they scroll, etc. All this and other behavioral metrics help you better understand visitors which help you improve user experience.

Other ways to analyze your website and collect data for analytics include CRM tool and marketing data. This data is always available and can be accessed easily. Your website should be the main data source for analytics. You need to track everything on your websites because this is the easiest way to understand your ideal customers' behavior.

3. Surveys and Interviews

Competitors and your own website provide you with a lot of data that you can use for analytics and decision-making but these two sources don't cover everything. There are times when you have to collect primary data using surveys, interviews, focus groups, and other data collection techniques.

This data is needed and useful for several reasons:

1. Understanding your target audience
2. Product testing and prototyping
3. Brainstorming and idea generation
4. Creating buyer personas
5. Marketing research projects

Nothing beats primary data for the fact that you contact the population that's appropriate. This helps you collect firsthand data from respondents of your choice.

For instance, if you are creating buyer personas and need information about your ideal customers' interests, hobbies, challenges, pain points, average income, social status, marital status, etc. you need to conduct surveys and structured interviews. This is the kind of information that you can't get from your competitors, website, or third-party research databases.

You can collect primary data in multiple ways:

1. Surveys
2. In-depth interviews
3. Structured interviews
4. Focus groups
5. Observations

Primary data collection is expensive and challenging. This is one reason why most small businesses and startups don't focus too much on primary data collection. However, it is something that you should never ignore especially if you intend to grow your business.

Why?

Because you get information from your target audience and customers directly. This type of data always works better than other types of data that you collect indirectly.

Why Relying Heavily On Google Analytics for Analytics Is a Big NO

I have to say that Google Analytics is a great tool that helps you with website analytics and lets you collect data on your website. But if you're relying only on Google Analytics for website analysis, you're making a big mistake.

Here is why.

First, GA is a great tool and it is not about how to *replace* it, but to show you that if GA is your only analytics tool, you're leaving a lot of money on the table every single day. You probably already heard/read these market insights:

1. Companies using analytics effectively have 126% profit improvement over competitors. (McKinsey)
2. Companies actively using data have 50% higher revenue growth. (Dell Global Technology Index)

We meet a lot of prospects who consider themselves to be among these companies because they have Google Analytics and a few analytics folks in-house. That makes our pitch at Air360 get the usual first welcome: *"Nah. Not interested, we got Google Analytics, thanks"* (of course they don't say it like this but that's the idea)

For many of them, they consider the analytics checkbox is already checked. Even better, sometimes it is checked for free (or at least, what they *consider* "for free").

Don't get me wrong, I don't blame them. After all, Google Analytics has been around forever and used by everyone from the small blog to Fortune 500 companies. For most people nowadays, Analytics = Google Analytics.

There's one question I like to ask these prospects: *"Why do you think companies like Uber, Netflix, etc. all have* **hundreds of people dedicated to analytics***? I mean why don't they simply use Google Analytics?"*

- Is it because they have too much money to spend?
- Is it because they have more complicated systems?
- Is it because they're just bigger?

Of course, the answer is no for each of these questions. It's just these companies understood they can't operate on gut feeling. The risk is just too big. On the other hand, analytics provides a reliable way to operate a business and saves a lot of time and potential mistakes that would cost millions.

The truth is, analytics, *when done right*, provides a strong competitive advantage for any business of any size.

So what do we mean by "done right"? While this is a question that would deserve a whole book, here are a few things on why only relying on Google Analytics for analytics will make you leave a lot of money on the table.

Here are 8 reasons why Google Analytics is simply not enough.

1. Google Analytics Doesn't Focus on the Most Important Part of Your Business: Your Customer

Users are considered as a simple number in your Google Analytics. But users are more than a number, believe it or not, they're real humans like you.

And there's a lot you can learn from your users or customers by being able to see how they actually behave on your website or in your app on a per-user basis. It's amazing what you can learn by analyzing user behaviors one by one. This can be usually done with user flows or session replays.

Unfortunately, you can't do any of these things with Google Analytics. So you can't really see and understand how specific users behave on your site and get valuable insights from it. You will just have to settle for aggregated and more than often, non-actionable data.

2. Google Analytics Doesn't Focus on User Activity

Google Analytics focuses on giving you macro KPI such as page views, sessions or bounce rate. However, it won't tell you much about how your users behave on your website. For instance, do first-time users find the products they want easily? How does your blog content contribute to your sales? What part of your homepage drives the most conversions?

These kinds of questions can't be answered easily with Google Analytics and if you can't really analyze what kind of actions your users perform on your website or app, it's impossible to measure how your marketing efforts, UX and content strategy improve your sales.

GA will tell you how many people entered/left your store and how much time they spent there but it won't tell you anything about the users who left without buying from you. Were they looking for something in particular they didn't find? Did they try to purchase and gave up? How many and what kind of products did they browse? Did they ask for help?

GA is a fairly good tool at giving you a conversion rate, but will miserably fail to tell you what made some users leave your website before completing a purchase or signup.

Google Analytics will give you a bounce rate but will fail to tell you what the user actually saw or did before bouncing. Google Analytics will show an increase in your conversion rate but will fail to explain why.

To sum it up, Google Analytics shows you the "what" but never tell about the "why".

And there's a big difference here:

Knowing the "what" makes you informed.

Knowing the "why" give you the power to know what to improve.

If you don't know the "why", you're leaving a lot of money on the table.

3. No Session Replay

Session replay is an awesome feature that makes you feel like you are sitting behind a user who is using your website. Watching these session replays feels like watching your favorite drama on Netflix, be prepared for laughs, scary, and funny moments.

If you don't have session replay, you're missing a big opportunity to improve your sales funnel and leaving money on the table every day.

Fun tip: Have your team binge watch a few session replays on Fridays, it will create fun moments and spark new ideas & discussions in your product team.

4. No Automation

Automation rocks. Want to send a customized greeting email to your website visitors coming from product hunt? Check.

Need to send a custom push notification to your users who are showing signs of churn? Check.

Reengage users who signed up but didn't use your killer feature yet? Mega-triple check.

Marketing automation is awesome as it makes you less busy while giving you superpowers. The more you automate, the more you can personalize your messaging, the higher you will profit.

If you're looking for an easy way to do more with less and you're not using automation already, you're missing out.

5. Google Analytics Doesn't Allow You to Look in the Past

If you want to record user events in GA, you need to have your engineers explicitly track what you might need in the future. The problem with this approach is that it is very hard to know what kind of data will be interesting in the future. Some useless events today might be gold for your business in the near future. Crystal ball anyone?

In order to prevent this, some analytics tools record every-thing for you. Yes, everything: Clicks, swipe, page change, scrolls, mouse events, touch, double tap, you name it.

The result is that you are 100% sure that you will never miss important data in the future. Not being able to do this is a terribly bad bet that might cost you a lot of money in the future.

6. Google Analytics is Actually Much More Expensive Than You Think (Even the "Free" Version)

Yes, Google Analytics is free, but if you do the math of how much time and money you and your team spend on Google Analytics every year, you would be very surprised. I won't even mention the money you leave on the table for all hidden actionable insights that Google Analytics won't find for you.

So I can't help myself but smile when I hear that "*Google Analytics is free*" from people who can't even tell how many hours they would spend per year on it. Much less how much money (or budget or time) it represents. Sometimes, I think it's better not to know. As they say, ignorance is bliss.

People often forget to consider is the total cost of ownership when buying software, do the math, it's never too late.

7. Google Analytics Doesn't Offer Any Support

Everything gets very complicated and time-consuming with Google Analytics when you want to do more than checking how many users, sessions or page views you got on a given period of time.

Since Google Analytics doesn't offer any support, you will have to rely on support forums and online help. It is an industry secret but a lot of GA users actually throw up the towel and stick with very basic analytics for this reason.

That is why a lot of companies offer Google Analytics consulting services. They're here to help Digital Marketing people get a correct GA setup and this is not rare to see this last for weeks or months.

Of course, you can be lucky enough to have strong Google Analytics skills in your team but these are very rare as Google Analytics is a much more complicated tool than it seems if you want to get actionable insights from it.

This leaves you with the difficult choice of paying a lot of money to get a useful Google Analytics setup or stick with a simple GA dashboard that will not yield not much to no value at all for your business.

8. It's Just a Tool

Delivering growth with analytics actually require several skills: UX, Data Science, SQL, Tech, Digital Marketing. Getting these skills in-house is a costly option if you are familiar with how much these resources cost nowadays. That is why we also offer a GrowthOps plan that is like having a complete analytics team on demand for a fraction of the cost.

If you want to collect accurate better data, increase your conversion rates and your sales, there are plenty of much better alternatives to Google Analytics out there. Air360.io is one of them.

The most important is to use a tool that checks all of the above features and will give you the data you need to measure and increase your conversions.

5

CHAPTER #3: HOW TO USE ANALYTICS?

You have collected a lot of data about your competitors, website, and via surveys and interviews, now you need to make sense of the data. Once you have the data, the analytics part kick starts.

There are numerous ways on how to use analytics practically for growing your business. This chapter covers the basics only. It will show you some of the best and most popular use cases of analytics.

1. Buyer Personas

Nothing beats buyer personas and their importance for your business success. It gets really hard to reach your target audience without having buyer personas.

So what exactly is this buyer persona and how you can create for your business?

HubSpot defines a buyer persona as:

"A buyer persona is a semi-fictional representation of your ideal customer based on market research and real data about your existing customers."

Buyer personas or customer avatars have one goal: To clearly define who your ideal customers are.

Buyer persona contains all the necessary information and data about your ideal customers including:

1. A fictional name
2. Designation
3. Interests and hobbies
4. Life challenges
5. Demographics
6. Background
7. Goals
8. Fears
9. Objectives

You can add other details too such as search preferences, preferred social network, the content type they like, where they spend time, and more. The idea is to better understand your ideal customers who will buy from you.

When you know your ideal customers, you can provide them with products they can't refuse, you can offer them with an experience they will love, you'll offer them content they will always love, and you'll do everything that they like. That's one amazing way to grow your customer base.

Buyer persona doesn't just help with marketing but they push your business in the right direction by telling you who your ideal customers are and what they expect from your business. This information is useful for all the departments and units throughout your business be it sales, finance, distribution, logistics, customer support, or any other.

How to Create a Buyer Persona for Your Business

Personas are amazing in what they deliver. Creating them is a bit tricky though as you have to rely heavily on primary data. Yes, buyer personas are solely based on primary data which means it is a direct application of analytics in business-settings.

Creating a buyer persona becomes easier if you know what you have to do. Here is how to do it step-by-step.

Step #1: Identify Target Audience

Finding the right people who will be interested in your product is one of the biggest challenges that a business faces. If you can find the target audience, your work is done. Selling becomes a piece of cake when you pitch your product to the right people.

Identifying the right people (target audience) is the first step towards buyer persona development. You need to create a rough sketch of your ideal customer who will purchase from you. For instance, if you're selling a weight loss supplement, your target audience is obese men and women. If you're selling gaming laptops, your target audience is gamers preferably teenagers. And so on.

In most cases, you don't target a single group. You'll sell weight loss supplement to men, women, women who gave birth to a child, celebrities, etc. You'll be targeting multiple segments and you need to identify all the target groups at this stage.

List all the target groups that might be interested in your product at some point in time. This is one area where competitor analysis will help you. Run your main competitor's website through a competitor spying tool like SpyFu, Ahrefs, or SEMRush and identify their target groups.

All the different target groups of your direct competitors are your target groups. You can identify these target groups by keywords they're targeting, by analyzing their ad campaigns, keywords they're using in their copy, and SERPs.

Step #2: Research

After you have identified all (or most of) target groups that you'll be targeting, you need to find more information about each target group. The information you already identified isn't enough. You need to dig deep. You need to know more about your target audience. This can be achieved by conducting interviews and surveys.

The idea is to do research about your target audience and target groups.

You need to conduct in-depth interviews with your primary target audience. Here are a few questions that you should ask to better understand your target audience:

1. *What are the biggest challenges that you're facing in your life?*
2. *What are the work-related challenges that you face on a daily basis?*
3. *Describe your personal demographics?*
4. *Tell me about your education, qualification, and professional experience?*
5. *Where do you see in life after five years?*
6. *What are your hobbies?*
7. *What is your biggest fear in life?*
8. *How often you use the internet?*
9. *Do you use social networking sites?*
10. *What's your favorite social media platform?*

The list can go on and on. You can add as many questions as possible. All the questions should be relevant and should help you get a better understanding of the respondent. Refrain from asking questions that provide you with data that you won't use or don't intend to use.

Yes, you need to ask product-specific questions as well just to get an idea of if the respondent actually belongs to your target group and should you really target this group. Since the product is already developed, you can't change it, however, you can target a different group of people so don't ignore product-related questions.

After you have conducted a few in-depth interviews with your target audience, you'll be in a better position to create a questionnaire with MCQs or a Likert scale survey. Surveys are cost-effective, easy-to-administer, and help you collect data from a fairly large sample.

The data you collected via interviews should be used as base to create a survey. Distribute the survey and collect more data for each target group. Conducting a survey after interviews isn't necessary, you can always skip it. But doing so will increase the reliability of the data.

It is recommended to conduct a large-scale survey to verify data collected through interviews. It will be of great help to you.

Step #3: Fill Buyer Persona Details

Finally, it's time to fill all the data into your buyer persona. You can create your own buyer persona from scratch or you can use a template. Hubspot offers a tool called Make My Persona that will help you create a buyer persona.

The idea is to have buyer personas that are the true representative of your target audience, target groups, and ideal customers. This is more important than graphical representation.

2. Segmentation

A buyer persona is just one practical form of analytics and what data can do for your business growth. Another amazing use of analytics is segmentation.

Let me give you an example.

John loves your app. As a 27-year-old gamer from Ohio with plenty of free time, John may not commit to an app quickly, but when he does find one that he likes he uses it daily.

Jane is unimpressed. She's an 18-year-old college student from New York. She seems to like its potential and used it for a few weeks, but after a month there was a slow and steady decline and once she was done she was done for good.

Jimmy is a 49-year-old trucker from California. He could not be less interested. He tried it for a day and left. He prefers to spend his time browsing YouTube for conspiracy theories.

John, Jane, and Jimmy all had very different experiences with your app or website. But they're also not the only ones. There are potentially thousands of Johns and Janes, and while you hope there are very few Jimmys, chances are there are thousands of those as well.

What is User Segmentation?

User segmentation is the process of categorizing users into segments that match some characteristic about them, whether it's:

1. Demographics
2. Behaviors
3. Location
4. Device
5. Interests

Instead of looking at all of the data of your users combined, you can split it into groups, like "males and females" or "married vs unmarried" or "millennials vs. boomers." It can also be behavior related, such as "used the recommended feature vs. didn't" or "abandoned shopping cart vs. made purchase."

There can be more than two segments to a group, but it helps that they all have some type of defining characteristic that is different between the groups.

Why Segment Users?

To understand why user segmentation is so important, we have to take a trip back to middle school math class. There, we were taught that "average," while easy to calculate, wasn't necessarily that useful for understanding the specifics about large groups.

- 10 people that bought 2 items each have an average of 2 items purchased per person.
- 9 people that bought 0 items and one person that bought 20 have an average of 2 items purchased per person.

In the former example, everyone is buying your products, and so your next step may be how to find new customers, or how to increase the number of items purchased, etc. In the latter, you want to figure out who made that 20 item purchase and find more of them.

But if you're looking at aggregate data (averages), you don't get to know which is which. Sure, you can drill down and figure it out in small doses, but how do you figure out the characteristics of your ideal customer? How do you determine their buying behaviors? How do you determine what you need to change to reduce dropout from the Janes and increase purchase power of the Johns?

Segmentation is what makes this possible. By splitting them into segments – for example, Janes and Johns, or recurring vs churning, etc. – you can more easily analyze their behavior, look for trends, see what campaigns work, and so much more, all in a way that give you real, tangible data that you can use to draw actionable conclusions.

Here are 6 ways how segmenting users can help your business.

1. Segmentation Lets You View Your Website through the Eyes of New Users

Imagine that Ashley, a runner, is visiting a website for the first time. She's eager to find a pair of shoes that comfortably fit her feet while she's running–ideally, something that will provide extra cushion for her feet after an injury.

Finally, her searching pays off! At last, she finds a website that seems to offer exactly the shoes she wants–or so she thinks. They offer several of the features she wants from her shoes. Unfortunately, she can't find any information about sizing. Do they run big or small? If she buys the wrong size, can she return them? Is the website reputable, or is she looking at a sham? Because the information she needs isn't readily available, she quickly clicks away from the website and ends up buying her shoes from a competitor.

Louis, on the other hand, is an experienced running shoe buyer, and he buys them from this website all the time. When he visits, he goes straight to the page he wants and knows exactly what size to order. He's familiar with the brand, so he doesn't have to worry about answering those difficult questions.

Do you have people like Ashley coming to your website, getting confused by the way you've arranged information or by your services? If you want to bring in new customers, you need to segment your data so that you can see exactly how different types of visitors respond to your website. This might include segmenting your data according to:

- Types of visitors (first-time versus returning)
- What brought users to the website
- What contacts the visitor has had with your website (your blog posts, for example)

When you segment your data, you can get a better look at how different types of customers respond to your website design—and, as a result, you can make changes to help it appeal to different types of users. You might discover, for example, that your website fails to convert new visitors, while repeat customers find it easier to use your website. On the other hand, you might discover that new customers are more likely to make a purchase than repeat customers, which means you may need to make other changes to your website's structure.

2. Segmentation Helps You Focus on Precisely What Users Want

DMA found that marketers see a 760% increase in revenue from email campaigns when they segmented their email lists. That's a huge increase—and with good reason! Segmented email campaigns allow you to deliver precisely the content that each user is looking for.

Imagine, for example, that Ashley is still looking for running shoes. She's joined the mailing list for a website that offers shoes and other athletic gear, hoping she'll get a welcome code or other discounts. She quickly starts receiving emails from the company, but they seem to be focused on marketing their football pads and cleats, not on running shoes. That's not at all what Ashley is interested in.

On the other hand, another company discovers that Ashley is looking for running shoes, so they send her emails specifically about shoes. They share information about choosing the right shoes for her feet, including testing her stride to learn whether her foot rolls in or out and how her foot strikes the pavement when she's running. Each email they send her, even if it isn't promotional, contains genuinely useful content. When they market other materials, its things that actually interest Ashley: running shorts, special lights for running in the dark, and belts that will help hold all her supplies, for example.

Which company is Ashley going to be most likely to buy from? Ashley might be intrigued by offers that the other company sends her, but at the end of the day, she's going to choose shoes from the company that's built up her trust. Once she's made her shoe purchase, she might be more likely to branch out and consider other options—like the belt or the light—but she wants to choose her shoes first. Segmented email marketing allowed the shoe company to provide her with the materials she really needed to make a buying decision.

3. Segmentation Helps Prevent Unnecessary Emails

It's not just about the emails you do send. It's also about the emails that you don't. Many customers join your mailing list primarily to get discounts or specific information about the products they use from your company. Unfortunately, only about **9% of sales emails** actually get opened. Customers will decide within the first couple of emails whether they want to continue opening emails from your company. If you regularly send out information that they find neither interesting nor useful, they may stop opening and reading your emails very quickly. In some cases, excessive emails may get you sent straight to the customer's spam box—or they might just unsubscribe altogether.

4. Return Shoppers Buy More than New Customers

Repeat customers make up only about 8% of visitors to most websites, but they deliver around 40% of your revenue. When a repeat customer checks out your products, you have a 60-70% chance of selling to them, while a new visitor has only about a 5-20% chance of making a purchase, depending on your industry and your products.

This makes customer retention a critical part of your marketing efforts.

Ultimately, a new customer has the potential to be worth 10 times their initial purchase to your company, but in order to take advantage of that, you must focus on keeping those customers and bringing them back. The good news is, the longer a customer is with your business, the better you can get to know them. You can learn about their buying habits: the types of purchases they want, the things that intrigue them, the promotions that are likely to bring them to check out your site. Then, you can segment your users according to those behaviors so that you can focus your campaign on providing the content that most interests each type of customer.

5. New Customers are Less Expensive than Repeat Customers

It costs seven times as much in terms of advertising dollars to acquire a new customer than it does to keep a repeat customer. Repeat customers already know your business and what you have to offer. You know what they want to purchase and how they prefer to connect with your brand. As a result, it costs less to keep those repeat customers–but you need to segment your lists to focus on those customers' needs.

6. Personal Customer Experiences Increase Sales Value

Let's take another look at Ashley's shoe-buying experience for a moment. Ashley has finally found a place to buy her shoes, which she replaces on a regular basis. She has a standing order, and she places it whenever her shoes start to wear out, but that's often the extent of her interaction with that store.

One day, she finds a new shoe store. This shoe store is eager to attract him as a new customer, so they send her a great discount for her first order–maybe even a discount on the brand of shoes she's already using. Even if it's a new brand, she's intrigued enough to make the switch. Ashley gets the shoes and discovers that they work just fine for her needs. Then, she starts receiving emails and other advertisements from the new shoe store. They seem to really know her: exactly the kind of shoe she likes, where she's located, and how her running is going. When Ashley decides to train for a race, the new store sends her training tips – and advertises some new, cool race gear that she can't wait to try out. When she's spending most of her time crunching data behind her desk during a difficult season at work, she gets content about how to stretch at the end of the day, and walking workouts that won't take up too much of her time.

Ashley is now loyal to the new shoe company. Not only that, when they send her specialized, targeted information about other products they offer, she's eager to try them out. She trusts the company and wants to see what else they offer – unlike her first company, which she used only for shoes. The difference? Simply a personalized customer experience.

Like Ashley, your customers want a personalized experience. They want to feel as though your company relates to and understands them. By segmenting your email campaigns, you can create a more personalized experience for every customer, which in turn will increase their value to your company.

The Value of Segmenting and a Tool That Handles It All

Data analysis rely heavily on user segmentation. It lets you better understand your audience and customer. Here is the thing: Not all users are equal.

Your audience comprises of different groups of people and you should treat them as such to get better insights. Segmentation is when you group data by a theme or category to make sure your analysis is more useful and actionable.

You can segment customers based on several variables such as buying behavior, usage, engagement, etc. There are unlimited variables that you can use to segment audience, users, and customers.

Let's look at two examples:

1. You have data that shows that all your customers like vanilla and chocolate ice cream equally.
2. You have data that shows women like vanilla and men like chocolate ice cream.

What data is more valuable?

Data in aggregate is useless data.

(·_·) You might say that data in aggregate is...

(·_·)>-

(_) aggravating.

The truth is that data viewed without segmentation is rarely usable.

Let's stick with the ice cream example. If all the data shows that people like chocolate and vanilla more than strawberry, you'd probably want to decrease strawberry and increase chocolate and vanilla production.

What if further analysis reveals that strawberry is the first choice for men over 55?

Now reducing the production of strawberry ice cream makes less sense. You have to adjust targeting and try selling it to the right segment to boost revenue.

How you can collect this type of data and how to segment customers based on variables that actually make sense?

The answer is Air360.

The ultimate goal of Air360 – and any good analytics tool – is to increase conversions. In order to increase the conversion rate, you need to understand how your audience uses your website and app.

Here's a more concrete example.

You're interested in measuring the bounce rate of your website. Analyzing the bounce rate for your entire audience is misleading. It blends data for those discovering your website for the first time with those that are returning visitors.

It includes misleading data, for example, spam bots or visitors from countries outside of your service.

It also has biases such as:

· Returning visitors tend to visit more pages and interact with your website more often than new visitors. This creates what's known as "survivorship bias," where you accidentally concentrate on visitors that made past the selection process while ignoring those that did not.

· Returning visitors may also travel through different paths and mediums compared to new visitors. Identifying the history or referral source that turn new visitors into returning visitors is not possible without reviewing your funnel.

The point is: You have to segment visitors based on their interaction with your website. The common variables include new and returning visitors.

You can segment your audience on the basis of several variables including:

1. Demographics
2. Landing Pages
3. Referral Sources
4. Location

5. Purchase history
6. Behavior
7. Psychographic

Let's assume, the data tells you that 3% of the visitors made a purchase:

1. Browsed handbags products: 1% purchase from you
2. Browsed swimwear products: 3% purchase from you
3. Came from one of your tweets: 8% purchase from you
4. Have read at least 5 blog posts from your blog: 12% purchase from you

What does this tell you?

It tells you that swimwear products are outperforming handbags. It tells you social media increases purchase rate dramatically. It also gives you a chance to ask further questions to go deeper into the analysis.

If this wasn't enough, consider the following statistics on segmentation and its benefits:

1. A study of 180 ecommerce stores (a total of over 33 billion visits) found that returning visitors represented only 8% of the total number of visits, but accounted for 40% of revenue, proving that with the right data-driven decisions a 2% increase in return shoppers would lead to a 10% increase in revenue.
2. First-time buyers are generally worth 10x as much as the value of their purchase. That is because once they make a purchase they are more likely to buy again. They're more likely to opt for the upsell.
3. It is 7x more expensive to acquire a new customer than to retain an existing customer. With segmentation, it

becomes possible to see how you can reduce customer acquisition cost and increase retention rate.

You can segment customers and your audience on the basis of several variables. It all depends on how you want to do it. For instance, ecommerce stores segment customers differently as compared to a SaaS company.

The best way to segment your audience is to identify variables that are important for your business and its growth. If, for instance, data shows you that users who log in to your app three consecutive days during free trial are the ones who will stick with your app for at least 100 days. You need to segment users based on usage and login activity.

This will help you identify users who haven't logged in so you can get in touch with them and convince them to log in to the app.

Collect data – as much as you can.

This helps you create segments. If you don't have data, you can't segment them.

RFM Model and What It Can Do For You

Segmenting sure makes your life easier and it helps you get better at analytics and decision-making but there is one problem...

Segmenting is an overwhelming task. Not all analytics tools do it perfectly. If your tool isn't flexible enough, you'll have to stick with the segments it creates. You won't be able to create your own segments.

Even if you get a chance to create segments, the big question is: Where to start?

I personally love the RFM Model which refers to recency,

frequency, and monetary. The customers are segmented based on these three variables.

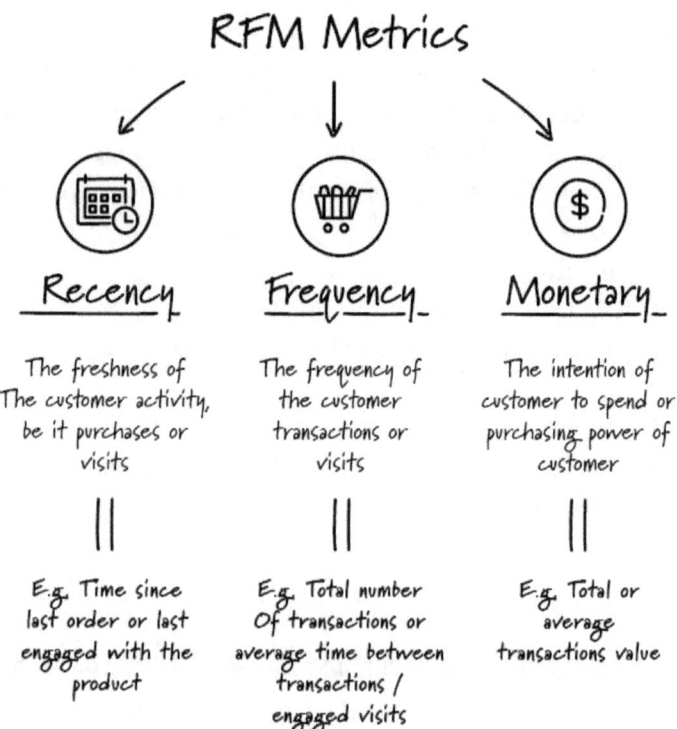

These are the three most critical variables that are directly linked to business growth. Recency is a measure of customer engagement and retention rate. Frequency and monetary determine customer lifetime value. Here is an overview of what each segmentation variable means:

Recency: Looking at how much time has passed since the last visited, performed an action, or made a purchase depending.

Frequency: It is the frequency of the purchase or visit within a specific time frame.

Monetary: Customer's purchasing power. How much spend so far and what's the total transaction value.

You can use RFM to assign tags to users and customers in order to segment and track purchase behavior. These tags represent a specific type of user that is related to where they fit.

For example, an "about to sleep" tag could be given to a user that appears to be fading and losing interest in your app. A "can't lose" tag may be valuable for a user that makes you a lot of profit but seems to have disappeared. A "high potential" tag is given to users that have all the data that matches your most profitable users, etc.

RFM makes it easier to identify customers by specific attributes (even more so if they are segmented properly) and then target them to improve conversion rate.

Let's look at an example.

Let me give you an example of how RFM works.

Let's assume you own a game app. Data analytics reveal that engaged users are involved in repeat purchases and they buy a lot of stuff. There are certain users who stop making in-app purchases gradually and they eventually stop using your app.

You don't want this to happen. You need to retain users and make them keep making in-app purchases.

Enter RFM...

With the RFM model, you can flag all such users with declining in-app purchases and look for ways to target them to regain their interest and improve repeat sales. You can use in-app popups that offer them with discounted items. Or, you can use in-app messages for engagement. You can conduct a survey and collect feedback on why they stop making in-app purchases all of a sudden?

The best thing you can do is persuade them to buy. This can be achieved with:

- Discounts
- Popup notifications
- Changing the app/website content
- Email outreach/marketing and more

You can then track whether they make the purchase, the effect it has on their app usage behavior, and more. This can be done easily with RFM.

The timing makes all the difference here.

By knowing more about individual users, you can figure out how to improve conversion rate and increase long-term revenue. You can create tags to segment users on the basis of chosen variables.

These tags are intuitive. What's better than understanding which customers have the highest potential and are most likely to become loyal customers?

The good thing is that the RFM model makes it easier to segment users without dealing with complex tasks. It generally does not require a data expert to understand how RFM can have value or what the value means when it is all put together.

This is one of its greatest advantages - not only is it generating information but it is doing so in a way that is easy to digest and use. It's a triple whammy.

What Google Analytics and Other Tools Leave Behind

Everything about RFM model and user segmentation is spot on with one issue.

Creating tags require a series of extremely complex calculations. What limits to set, how to move customers from one segment to another, how to quantify qualitative variables, and so on.

The worst part: You cannot create an RFM model in Google Analytics.

Let's admit it: Google Analytics is NOT made for RFM and cannot handle the requirements that make RFM meaningful.

One of the challenges is that Google Analytics is not the appropriate tool for RFM. Here is why:

- Google Analytics doesn't track individual users. It's hard to identify how many times a particular visitor has visited your website. You'll see an accumulated value of *Returning Visitors* but dig deep and understand more about these returning visitors.
- It's fairly complex to use tagging with Google Analytics. The tag system by Google isn't one of the best, I'm sure you know it. When you can't tag users, you don't get individual-level data.
- Google Analytics doesn't calculate RFM and cannot do it in real-time. If you're interested in doing so with GA, you have to do it manually by doing all the calculations yourself.
- Google Analytics doesn't accurately calculate all visits, interactions, and more. It doesn't provide you all the information about visitors such as interests, salary, psychographics, and more.

In fact, when you use Google Analytics for RFM, it creates more issues than helping you solve your problem. GA doesn't support funnel creation, it primarily tracks users on the basis of click activity, and it is not automated.

You can't get all the information from GA about important metrics in the RFM model that actually matter. For instance, you can't measure CLV, you can't identify user behavior on your site, there isn't mouse tracking feature, you can't segment returning visitors, and more.

You get the idea, right?

Google Analytics isn't your best choice for RFM. In fact, if you're interested in true data analytics, Google Analytics is the least helpful tool (*Read this article for more details*). It should be surprising but it is a fact.

According to Angela Bowman:

"Google Analytics excels in telling you the beginning and end of a visitor's journey, but the middle gets a little fuzzy."

It provides you a snapshot of your website but not the data that you can use for decision-making.

After all, it's free so you can't expect a lot.

3. Decision-Making

Businesses don't always make the best decisions.

They spend thousands of dollars on magazine ads seen by a few hundred but spend only a few dollars on social media seen by thousands.

They spend tens of thousands of dollars on upgrading to fancier signs and decorations around the office but spend only a few dollars on employee wellness and productivity improvements.

They spend hundreds of thousands of dollars on Steve, and Steve is terrible.

Meanwhile, they spend nothing at all on analytics, preferring instead to make decisions based on gut and experience and magic 8-balls and Ouija boards.

The truth is: We live in a time with outstanding access to information. Never before has any business been capable of accessing this much data – this much of a wealth of information about customers, sales, conversions, and more – all in ways that are also cost-efficient and intuitive.

Modern web and app analytics software makes it possible to collect, measure, and analyze an abundance of data so detailed that it can be easily used to drive better business decisions.

The question is HOW?

Here is an example of how Starbucks uses analytics for decision-making:

Impressive, right? But there is more...

Check out how brands like Ralph Lauren, True Religion, and Lucky Brand use analytics for decision-making:

RALPH LAUREN, LUCKY BRAND AND TRUE RELIGION

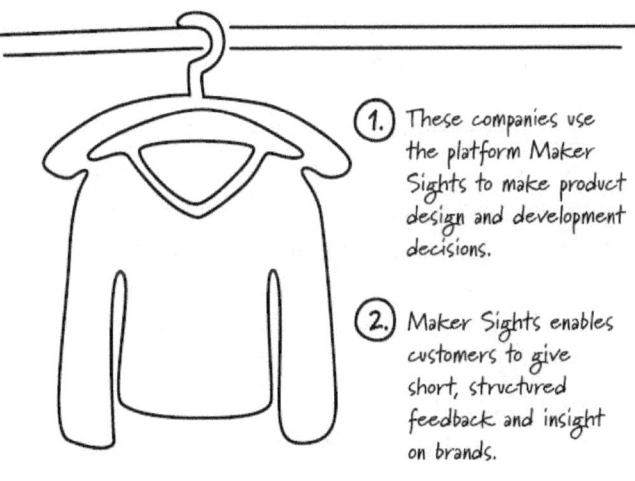

1. These companies use the platform Maker Sights to make product design and development decisions.

2. Maker Sights enables customers to give short, structured feedback and insight on brands.

3. The retailers apply sales data and machine learning to the feedback to minimize markdowns, take advantage of top-selling products, inform product design, and increase gross margins.

Analytics will always help you in decision-making, especially predictive analytics irrespective of your industry whether it be retail, manufacturing, oil and gas, banking, ecommerce, or any other.

You have to put all the data you have collected (and are still collecting) about competitors and customers to use. If you're using the right tools and you're collecting data from your website and across all customer touchpoints, you're heading in the right direction. Your decisions will be powered by analytics naturally.

4. User Experience (UX)

A Forrester study found that offering great UX can increase conversions by 400%. We all agree on the importance of UX in a website's design, its outcomes, and benefits. One of the best things about analytics is that it lets you improve UX.

Steve Krug says:

"Your website should be self-evident, obvious, and self-explanatory."

The users don't have to '*think*'.

When users have to think (and decide) as to what they should do (next), that's a UX failure.

Leaving something (or anything) on visitors, expecting that they will 'obviously' know what to do because it's too common, is a UX mistake that can cost your business a lot.

What happens when you make UX mistakes?

It increases the bounce rate, it reduces conversions, and increases churn. And improving UX can increase conversions by 400%.

Analytics help you a lot in improving UX. Not only does it help with issue identification but analytics also helps you investigate those issues and fix them.

UX Bug Identification with Analytics

If you're tracking your website with a behavioral analytics tool like Air360, you'll be able to find issues in UX that are restricting users from converting. For instance, scroll tracking will show you what's the part of the page that visitors spend most of the time and where they don't spend any time at all. This information alone can be used to tweak the elements that don't get attention from visitors.

A free tool like Google Analytics won't provide you with all the details you need to identify UX issues. It will, for instance, show you exit pages which are the pages on your website from where visitors leave your website. You can't change all the exit pages instead you need to specific information on what elements on these pages are causing visitors to leave.

This granular tracking is what a tool like Air360 does. You get to know how visitors interact with each individual page, what they do, where they click, how much they scroll, and so on.

Based on all the data, you can identify UX issues.

Not sure how to do it? Here is a simple rule for identifying UX bugs:

1. Create goals or conversion objectives. What you expect from each page on your website and what action you want visitors to take when they're on a specific webpage or a landing page.
2. If the majority of the visitors aren't taking the desired action, there is an issue that needs to be addressed.

It gets easier if you're using right tracking tools to measure everything on and off your website.

Once an issue has been identified, it further needs to be

69

investigated. Analytics will help here too. If visitors aren't converting on a landing page that you just created, is it due to a design-related issue? Is it a technical issue? Are you sending irrelevant traffic to the landing page? Is there a mismatch between the offer and the ad copy?

And so on...

Investigating the issue will become a challenging task if you aren't tracking with a decent analytics tool. An analytics tool will show you clearly what's happening and why it's happening. It will help you investigate any issue that you face in terms of UX (or otherwise).

UX Mistakes to Avoid

Some of the common yet costly UX mistakes are discussed in this article along with steps on how to avoid these mistakes.

1. Popups

Popups are controversial.

Google doesn't like them and announced that it will penalize websites that use intrusive popups that restrict people from accessing the content.

Sumo analyzed 1,754,957,675 popups (*this figure shows popups are used extensively*) and found that they work. The average conversion rate of popups is around 4% which can go as high as 40% when popups are personalized.

So marketers are still using popups because it works.

And the debate continues...

However, popups aren't bad.

The way how you use popups make them bad. When your

popup doesn't ruin UX, it's fine to use it. If it restricts website visitors from accessing content, that's a lethal UX mistake.

The thing is: There is a very fine line between popups that don't hurt UX and popups that hurt UX.

Google clearly distinguishes intrusive from non-intrusive popups. It's obvious that when you block a visitor's view with a popup (or anything else), it won't be appreciated. At least, I don't.

If you're using popups that cover full-screen and block visitor's view, you're ruining UX.

Solution

Fixing this UX mistake is easy.

Follow Google's guidelines. Google told you what you should do and how to use popups without hurting UX.

In fact, you should use popups to improve UX. Here is how to do it.

1. Don't use entry popups.
2. Use popups that don't cover the entire screen. Keep them small.
3. Use personalized popups that are relevant to visitor's previous interaction with your website and are consistent with the content of the page.
4. Create engaging and valuable popups that visitors will love interacting with.
5. Allow visitors to close the popup with a single click. Make close button prominent.

2. Complexity

Sebastian Tan wrote an interesting article on how PayPal has a poor UX. He tried withdrawing money from his PayPal account and the field wasn't user-friendly.

In fact, it was complicated. Entering the amount, deleting it, and deleting part of the entered amount was messy.

What does this show?

UX mistakes are common and even big companies make them. It is against the basics of UX. It makes users think. They have to find their way. Complex navigation, complex design, complex user flow, and complex hierarchy won't help website visitors.

The Bolden contact form isn't user-friendly. It's complex because you cannot find it, the font color and the background blends, and form border isn't visible clearly.

Creating problems for visitors instead of facilitating them never works.

Solution

Replace complexity with simplicity. Make it easy and simple for users to do what they want to do.

Instead of letting users find their way, guide them.

The easiest technique to remove complexity is to follow Brady Bonus's three-step method to removing complexity which he derived from John Maeda's laws of simplicity:

1. **Reduce** thoughtfully everything that's not needed. Stick with what's necessary.
2. **Organize** what is left after reduction.
3. **Prioritize** by defining a clear hierarchy.

Reduction, organization, and prioritization will lead to a simplified UX.

3. Ignoring Mobile

Perhaps the biggest UX mistake is ignoring mobile users. Not having your website optimized for mobile will ruin UX. Statistics show that 52.2% of all website traffic in 2018 was generated through mobile.

This means 47.8% of traffic is generated from all other sources including desktop, tablets, iPads, Kindle Fire, and other devices.

And mobile traffic converts quickly. Almost 70% of mobile searches result in an action on the website within an hour.

According to Google, a non-mobile friendly website will hurt a brand's reputation. As much as 48% of users feel frustrated when they visit a website that's not mobile-friendly.

You cannot afford to have a poor UX on your mobile site.

Solution

You have to admit that mobile is different than desktop.
   1. Mobile screen is small
   2. Mobiles have touchscreens which are different than keyboards
   3. People mostly use mobile with a single hand.

With this in mind, you need to create UX. It should handle the small screen size, it should be designed to support the touchscreen, and it needs to be created for people who use mobile with one hand.

There are several best practices that you can use to improve mobile UX:

- Utilize above the fold. Make sure it has a CTA and a short form.
- Avoid popups especially ones that cover the mobile screen.
- Add a link to search in the primary menu so visitors can use the search engine to find what they're looking for.
- Offer live chat on mobile so that expert agents offer assistance to potential customers right away.
- Add links to help section in the menu. This will help visitors solve their problems themselves.

UX improvement is a continuous process. It's common to create mistakes related to UX, and it's not a problem. The problem is when you can't identify your mistakes which means you won't be able to solve them. It is, therefore, essential to find UX mistakes so you can take appropriate action.

When you tweak UX, measure its impact with split testing. Does change improve any metric? Does it improve the conversion rate? If it doesn't change a thing (or has a negative impact), switch back.

UX changes should be data-driven.

5. Conversion Rate Optimization (CRO)

A related but different concept to UX is CRO. Everything at the end of the day is all about conversions be it your sales funnel, PPC, paid-to-trial, or email signups. CRO is one thing that you can't measure and/or improve without analytics. It is all about analytics – and nothing else.

CRO is the process of making people take action when they

visit your website or a landing page. CRO process involves multiple stages including:

1. Research
2. Hypotheses development and prioritizing
3. Testing and experimentation
4. Evaluation

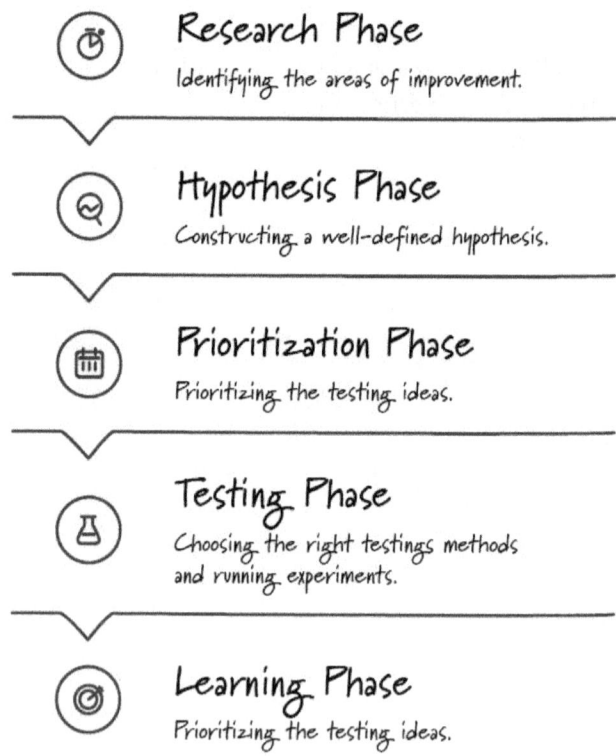

Research Phase
Identifying the areas of improvement.

Hypothesis Phase
Constructing a well-defined hypothesis.

Prioritization Phase
Prioritizing the testing ideas.

Testing Phase
Choosing the right testings methods and running experiments.

Learning Phase
Prioritizing the testing ideas.

The research phase is all about analytics. If you're tracking conversions and have an analytics tool in place, you'll be able to create and test hypotheses that will show you what elements on a specific page are ruining conversions and how to fix them.

Best CRO Strategies Powered by Analytics

When you'll implement your analytics tool, it will start collecting data. The data needs to be analyzed. The analysis and reporting are also handled by the tool.

You can generate reports which you can use for measuring conversions. The way how you analyze data and use it for CRO is an essential growth component. The analytics tool doesn't tell you what element you have to test rather it will just show you the data in an easy-to-understand way.

How you interpret data and how you hypothesize is all up to you.

Here are a few CRO strategies to increase conversions and growth by looking at data from your analytics tool.

Identify Weaknesses

A lot of advanced analytic tools like Air360 will show you weak areas of your website or app that needs special attention. Other tools won't show you what needs to be improved.

For instance, Google Analytics will only show you data and won't tell you weak areas of your website that needs attention. Even if it shows you weak areas, it doesn't tell you what steps you need to take for improvement.

Air360, on the other hand, will show you full insights and weak areas of your app and website you're tracking with it. You'll also get to see what steps to take for improvement.

So it depends on what tool you're using.

Boost Website Load Speed

Site load speed is a critical UX factor. If you notice an increase in bounce rate, the first thing that you need to check is your website's loading speed.

Why?

Because if your website doesn't load fast, visitors are more likely to leave your website. Statistics show that people wait up to 10 seconds for a website to load. If it doesn't load in 10 seconds, they will leave.

Patience of mobile web users

How long are users willing to wait for a site to load
before they abandon the page? The following graph
seeks to answer this question.

Observation: Most participants in the survey would
wait 6-10 seconds before they abandon pages.

1-5 Seconds	6-10 Seconds	11-15 Seconds	16-20 Seconds	20+ Seconds
3% 16%	30%	16%	15%	20%

3% of those surveyed said that they would wait less than
one second for a page to load before abandonment.

What you should do is use Google's PageSpeed Insights to
check your website's load time and take appropriate actions
as suggested by the same tool to improve speed.

Read this post for step-by-step instructions.

Remember, when a lot of people leave your website, it means

visitors don't even enter your sales funnel. It's frustrating be-cause it will ruin your entire funnel and will reduce conversions on all the stages eventually hurting growth negatively.

Test Your Forms

This is related to the Interest Stage of your funnel. When a visitor is interested in your app, he will take the pain to fill the form so you can contact further.

In other words, your lead generation form is what makes or breaks the deal.

Don't let form ruin conversion rate. You need to optimize form to improve conversions. Here are a few tips to do it:

- Reduce form fields. Only collect information that's relevant.
- Keep the form as short as possible.
- Use dropdown lists so that users don't have to type every-thing.
- Make your form responsive.
- Validate form entries in real-time so as to notify users of errors right as they fill the form.

Have a Next Step

Do you have web pages that lead nowhere?

A web page that doesn't guide visitors as to what step they have to take next will increase funnel leakages. When a visitor doesn't know what to do next, he will (most likely), leave your website (and funnel) forever.

Interlink web pages. Remove pages that don't have a purpose. If it has a purpose, link page to its goal so visitors can reach where they're supposed to reach.

Work on Your Profitable Referral Sources

Segmentation allows you to see the profitability of each referral source along with demographic data. Review your referral sources to see if one methodology is thriving, calculate the number of hits that you can generate with an increase in investment, and then put more resources into that.

Understand Your Customers

It is critical to know who your best customers are.

You can use data provided by the analytics tool to better understand your customers and their behavior. Avoid the guesswork and let data help you define the characteristics of your ideal customers.

6. Customer Support

Did you know: 56% of customers don't mind sharing their information (including personal data) with a company in exchange for better customer services? In another survey, 72% of businesses reported that analytics is best used to improve the customer support experience.

Yes, analytics and customer support are intertwined. Your job gets easier because consumers, on average, don't hesitate to share their personal information with a company if they expect that they will get better and personalized customer support services. It can't get easier than that.

We already discussed how analytics can help you improve

customer experience but don't confuse customer experience with customer support. Customer experience matters throughout your business across all the channels and touchpoints. For instance, customer experience is important when a visitor is browsing your website, is visiting your local store, is following you on social media, etc.

Customer support is specifically about everything related to customer services that you offer when a customer reaches you for help. In this sense, customer support is way more critical for your business growth as compared to customer experience. A customer may contact support in case of an issue and if you don't deal well and don't offer personalized services (in the absence of analytics), that'd lead to a disaster.

You don't like losing customers. No business does.

Analytics play a crucial role in customer support and how you deal with your customers. Let me give you an example.

I recently contacted my cellphone carrier. I introduced myself and told the agent that my sim card isn't working after I have received a duplicate sim card from their outlet. I was getting invalid sim card error. And guess what the agent asked me: Where did you get this sim issued?

I was like: You should have this information in your system. He replied: I'll check sir.

And then he asked me again: What is the problem you're facing?

I was getting irritated because I already told the whole story. The support agent was least interested in helping me and he wasn't using his system and existing data on why I issued a sim card, who I'm, where I got the sim card issued from, and so on.

Having worked in the customer support department of a leading cellular network, I know that all these (and other) details are available with the agents.

That's how you ruin customer support and irritate customers when you don't use analytics. The customers expect to get answers. If you have shared your birth year with a company once and they ask you again, you'll definitely feel bad. You told them something and they're not using their system to check your data rather they're asking you again.

Things get worse because you end up making these silly mistakes with customers who are already frustrated with your company.

So what you can do?

Get organized. Use a CRM tool of your choice (e.g. Zoho) as it will solve half of your customer related issues. Use a customer support tool like Zendesk.

The thing is: You already have details and data about your customers. You need to organize it and equip your customer support staff with the right tools so they can access customer data immediately and respond appropriately.

This is why you need powerful customer support and ticketing tool. Get one today and start making sense of the data that you already have.

Conclusion

These were some of the (many) instances where analytics will help you grow your business. When analytics start pushing your business in the right direction, you need to track your performance and figure out how to improve it further. Tracking performance can be done by measuring and monitoring the right metrics. This is what is covered in the next chapter.

6

CHAPTER #4: MEASURING WHAT MATTERS

This chapter is all about measuring growth. You could be doing an exceptionally great job with analytics but if you aren't using it to grow your business, what's the point?

You have already covered everything about analytics, now is the time to understand about growth, performance, and how analytics will help with both.

Analytics measures a lot of variables. Not all of these variables and metrics are important for your business. Similarly, you can generate several kinds of reports once you have the data. The metrics that are important for your business might not be important at all for another business in the same industry.

When Intercom was started, it used to track its performance using traditional SaaS metrics like trial-to-paid and recurring revenue. Soon they realized that these metrics weren't showing them the true picture. These metrics didn't tell them what features users love, how was the customer experience, etc. They started tracking other metrics that showed them a better picture of their company.

Being a SaaS company, Intercom was using different metrics to track its performance than most of its competitors. If you're in the same industry or even if you're competitors, it isn't necessary to use exact same metrics to track performance.

So the first rule is to choose your own metrics to make more sense of the analytics and data. Even if you're tracking everything with a great analytics tool but if you aren't measuring metrics that are relevant to your business, it won't make much of a difference. Everything will be wasted.

This chapter will cover metrics that define your company's success and the metric that you should track with analytics. Before moving towards the metric, it is essential to understand metrics and Key Performance Indicators (KPIs) so that you can better understand how this is linked to analytics.

1. KPIs and Metrics

Key Performance Indicator (KPI) and performance metrics are the two terms that are most underrated and don't get due importance (and respect) from businesses. If you want to grow your business and if you're interested in pushing it in the right direction, you should know how to measure performance and how to check if your business is actually moving in the right direction.

KPIs and metrics help you track and measure performance and growth. You get to know if your business is moving in the right direction.

By definition, KPI is a measure of how well a business is meeting its both operational and strategic goals. Investopedia defines KPIs as quantifiable measures that a business uses to gauge its performance over time.

Key Performance Indicators
Definition and Examples

A quantifiable measure a company uses to determinate how well it's meeting operational and strategic goals.

A customer support team might measure the average on-hold time for customers

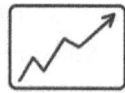

A sales team might track new revenue

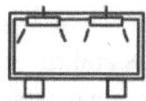

A marketing group will look at the contribution of marketing generated sales leads

Human resources will look at employee engagement

Other areas of the business will look at the efficiency of processes

KPIs vary greatly by department so your sales team might have KPIs defined in terms of sales generated in a month while your human resource department might track its KPIs in terms of employee engagement.

KPI is a performance indicator that lets you measure the

performance of your business, different departments, projects, and tasks. A metric, on the other hand, is a number that actually tracks the performance. Metrics are static that provide you information about a specific task such as the number of website visitors or average session duration.

Both metric and KPI are used interchangeably. These two terms are closely related but are different. KPIs define and track performance at the strategic level and are aligned with organizational goals while metrics are static, easy-to-understand, and activity-based.

Metrics vs. KPIs – A Comparison

Metrics	KPIs
Metrics provide information that can be digested.	KPIs offer comparative insights that guide future actions.
Metrics are extracted and organized by activity or process.	KPIs are initiated by high-level decision markers.
Metrics can be viewed historically, but do not identify future action.	KPIs incorporate Goals and Objectives.
Metrics are static, and once extracted do not change.	KPIs can be evaluated and reset over time using the SMART methodology.

Metric is a measurement or unit which doesn't make sense in isolation. It can only be understood when it is linked to KPI. Here is an example.

Your analyst sends you this email one fine morning:

"*Dear Sir,*

I'm pleased to inform you that we have increased the conversion rate of our ecommerce store by 15% and now 30 out of every 100 customers convert at our store. This was achieved last week and from this week onwards, we will continue to see a 30% conversion rate.

Thank you."

You forward the same email to your boss expecting a raise. But your boss replies unexpectedly with the following email:

"Dear XYZ,

The numbers are interesting but our objective for the current year was to increase organic traffic to our store to 50,000 visitors a month by the end of December. I don't see how the conversion rate is relevant to this objective?

As I can see, the organic traffic has consistently declined in the past 3 months and we are receiving less than 30,000 visitors a month.

Please focus on the objective and share the same with your team.

Regards,

The Boss"

Your team was tracking a metric (conversion rate) while the KPI was organic traffic. While the conversion rate is a decent metric but if it isn't aligned to your business's KPI, it won't be helpful at all.

This is what exactly happened in the example.

KPI is always driven by business objectives and is created by senior management and it targets key performance areas. KPIs provide your business and teams with the direction where they have to move.

How to Create KPIs for Your Business

One major difference between KPIs and metrics is that metrics are already defined while KPIs need to be defined rather created specifically. For instance, customer churn rate is a standardized metric that's already defined. You don't have to define it specifically for your business.

This isn't the case with KPIs. You have to create KPIs for your business to measure performance and to communicate your goals and objectives so that everyone knows what they have to do.

You need to create SMART KPIs that will make everything easier and under control. A SMART KPI is: Specific, Measurable, Achievable, Realistic, and Timely.

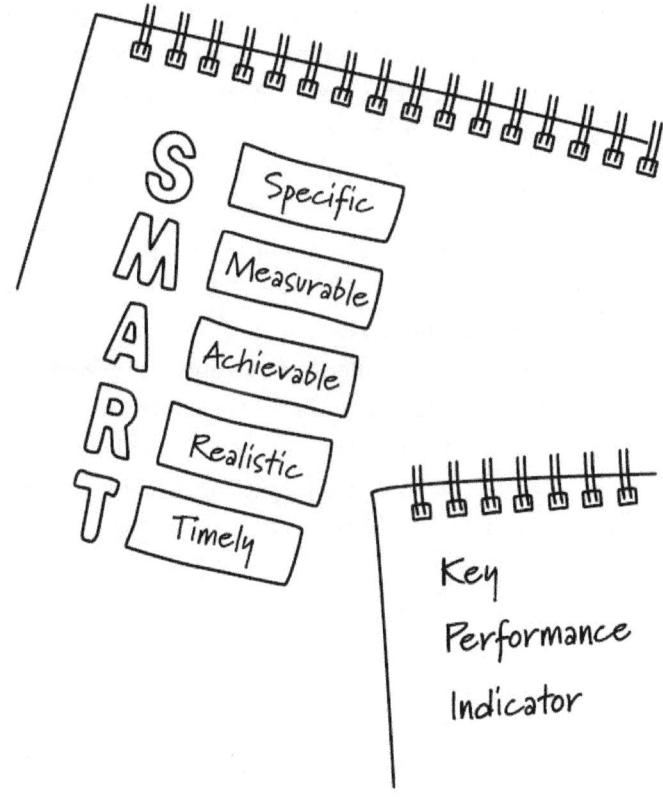

Here is an example of a KPI that isn't smart: *Increase in revenue.*

Now here is a SMART KPI: *Increase revenue by 10% in a year.*

Do you see the difference?

The SMART KPI is:

1. Specific with exact details.

2. It is measurable. You can measure an increase in revenue.
3. It is achievable because an increase of 10% in revenue in a year is fairly reasonable for most of the businesses.
4. It is realistic. You aren't asking too much from your team.
5. It has a time-frame attached to it. You're not giving unlimited time duration to achieve the objective.

In this SMART KPI, revenue is a metric that will be used to determine the success of the KPI but it isn't the only metric that will be used to gauge performance.

Based on this KPI, departments and teams will create their own goals which will be tracked by metrics. For instance, the marketing department will set its own goals to achieve the KPI. These goals will be tracked using marketing metrics. The sales team will use its own metrics to track its performance. And so on.

KPIs and metrics go hand in hand.

2. The North Star Metric

There are tons of metrics that you can use to track the performance of your business and to check its growth. There are fair chances that you might end up tracking an inappropriate metric. This will ruin your business growth and you'll be left far behind than your competitors.

It is critically essential that you choose the right metrics to grow your business and to ensure everyone in your company clearly understand that one metric. This is where the North Start Metric comes into action.

What is the North Star Metric?

It is the metric that captures your product's core value that it delivers to the customers. This metric has the potential to grow your business exponentially.

In simple words, it is the metric that your entire business, departments, teams, and individuals focus on to achieve sustainable growth. For instance, your marketing team should have a goal to generate leads and your sales team will be interested in generating sales. Both marketing and sales teams have different objectives.

With NSM, however, a single metric is followed by all the teams and everyone concentrates on the NSM and the business works as a unified whole and moves in the right direction that's best for business's growth.

Let me give you an example.

Facebook's North Star Metric is *Active Users (daily and monthly)*. Facebook is all about its users, it's a social network and it will go bankrupt if people stop using it. So what they have focused on is active users – the more the better.

Facebook's NSM is clearly visible on its Company Info page.

The key statistics include information on daily and monthly active users. This is the metric they are interested in.

The NSM is customer-driven. It is focused on the value that your product delivers to the customers. So Facebook's primary product is its platform and users stick with it due to the value they get from the platform.

Now it isn't necessary to state your business's North Star Metric on the company's page. You don't have to do it. However, it has to be communicated clearly so all the teams can move in the right direction.

Once you know the NSM, it becomes the center of all business activities and everything else revolves around it. It becomes your business's BIG goal.

Your employees know what their business is all about and what is expected of them.

Why Your Business Needs It

So what's so special about the North Star Metric?

Why you should care?

Why not go without it?

Well, there are quite a few amazing benefits that businesses get from the NSM which no other metric provides.

It doesn't mean that the North Star Metric is some kind of silver bullet that will change everything overnight. Of course, not. It is a metric which can be misleading, like any other metric. It can be misused. It can be problematic at times.

However, when compared to other metrics, it outperforms big time. Here are a few major benefits that make it better than its counterparts.

1. Sustainable Growth

The NSM is all about growth and this is what makes it better than other metrics.

LogMeIn shifted to NSM and it started growing exceptionally, and today it is a $6 billion company.

Focusing on the NSM will put your business on the right track and it will continue to grow. It becomes the centralized metric that all the teams try to achieve.

Its focus is nothing but growth.

2. Outcome-Focused

It is focused on delivering value to the customers and to retain customers which makes it an outcome-focused metric.

It's linked to customers, what makes them happy, and what makes them stick with your business. Additionally, it is a generalizable metric that all departments and teams can follow.

It's a business metric and not just any departmental metric.

3. One Goal

All the employees and teams clearly understand the NSM and they know what's expected of them. Even if their primary goal isn't directly related to the NSM (such as copywriting, designing, finance, etc.), they will still be able to see how their work adds value and helps their business achieve success.

Everyone knows what their business is all about and how to measure success. This makes it easier for your workforce to figure out how their work impacts business success.

4. Team Alignment

According to Sean Ellis, one of the best aspects of the NSM is that it significantly improves the team and departmental alignment. All the teams across your company will focus on one and only one thing: The North Star Metric.

This alignment means a lot for businesses. Research shows that companies with well-aligned sales and marketing teams have 38% higher sales win rates and 36% higher customer retention rate as opposed to companies with poorly aligned sales and marketing teams.

Imagine having all of your teams aligned and working together to achieve one goal.

5. It is Simple

The NSM is simple by nature for two reasons.

First, it is a company-wide metric so it has to be kept simple so everyone understands it. For instance, Facebook's *Active Users* is a very simple metric that non-Facebook users can understand with extreme ease.

Second, it describes the value customers get from your product so it cannot be something hard to understand. I mean, if you cannot explain in one or two words the core value your product delivers, you need to tweak your product.

The value your product offers has to be simple enough so you can explain what it is that you're offering.

3. Metric-Analytics Linkage

You know what a metric is, how it is different from KPI, and how you can identify NSM for your business – great.

Not all the metrics are considered growth metrics, you have to pick your NSM very carefully. Ask yourself: Is it a growth metric? If you'll track this metric and focus on it, will it lead to growth?

Your answer needs to be a big YES...

So we have talked a lot about metrics, it is time to understand how analytics fit here.

What if I tell you that metrics are all about analytics? All metrics are driven by analytics. Think of any metric: Average session duration, organic traffic, conversion rate, bounce rate, recurring revenue, churn rate, etc. You can't find any of these without data.

You need an analytics tool to track your preferred metric. Can you measure organic traffic, unique visitors, and top search keywords without using Google Analytics? Absolutely not.

You need an analytics tool (a powerful one) to measure metrics and thus KPI. You can't track the North Star Metric without analytics tool.

Let's assume your NSM is to ensure new signups use your app for at least 9 days because you know that once a user sticks with your app for 9 days, the churn probability reduces by 65%. Once you have set the NSM, the next big thing is to measure retention, activity level, and churn rate. You need an analytics tool (e.g. Air360) that will track churn rate and will intimate you right on time when a user is about to churn (based on activity level) so you can take appropriate action (e.g. retention call) to retain the user.

No matter what NSM you have selected for your business, you'll always need an analytics tool to track NSM. This makes metric-analytics a couple that's a must for business growth.

What Analytics Tools to Use

If you're thinking about Google Analytics, I have to stop you. We have already discussed a lot about Google Analytics in this book. It is a great tool which is free but it is definitely not one of the robust tools that will track everything for you.

You have to accept it.

I'm not saying that you shouldn't use it, of course you should. It is a great free resource that tells you a lot about your website and its traffic. What I'm saying is that you can't and shouldn't rely completely on Google Analytics if you're serious about analytics and if you want to grow your business.

So what analytics tool you should use?

The simple answer is: *Use a tool that accurately measures the NSM.*

At Air360, we use artificial intelligence to predict churn which makes our tool best for SaaS. Any business that's focused on reducing churn, Air360 is its best bet. In this case, Google Analytics won't be a good fit because it doesn't track churn rate.

Talking about Air360, it has a lot of features that make it better than any tracking tool that you'll find out there. It has the potential to track metrics that most of the other tools don't. Here are some of the best Air360 features that make it an awesome tool:

1. It tracks the activity of the users on both mobile and desktop. You can view all the actions that a user takes on your website.

2. It monitors scrolling and shows you how much time each user spends at the top, middle, and bottom of the page.

3. It creates segments on full autopilot based on user actions and behavior. This segmentation helps you in targeting especially when you integrate Air360 with other tools like CRM.

4. It comes with a powerful dashboard where you can generate reports of your choice.

5. Each individual is tracked individually with all the details including scroll data, visit history, page visits, actions taken, and complete behavioral analysis.

6. You can integrate Air360 with hundreds of third-party apps directly and via Zapier.

7. It offers you a lot of other features that you'll find with other leading analytics tools. Click here to read how Air360 compares to other analytics tools like Heap, Mixpanel, Google Analytics, Hotjar, etc.

Should you only use a single analytics tool?

No.

You can use multiple analytics tools. Again it comes down to what you're tracking. If you're interested in detailed heatmaps, you should try Crazy Egg. The more tools you use, the better. Because each tool tracks data on different metric and at the end of the day, you get a lot of data and reports that help you in making more informed decisions.

When using multiple analytics tools, make sure that you don't use tools that track similar metrics. This won't help much. Refrain from spending resources on such tools. In order to help you get started, here is a list of leading analytics tools:

1. Air360 (Behavioral analytics)
2. Google Analytics (Website traffic analytics)
3. Heap (Product analysis and CRO)
4. Mixpanel (Product analytics)
5. Hotjar (Heatmaps and visitor recording)
6. Crazy Egg (Heatmaps and A/B testing)
7. Click Meter (Link and conversion tracking)
8. VWO (A/B testing tool)
9. Sisense (Business intelligence and analytics platform)
10. Clear Analytics (Excel analytics tool)

Need more tools? A quick Google search will show you tons more but it is recommended to choose an appropriate analytics tool from the list above and move from there.

CHAPTER #5: THE ANALYTICS RECIPE: ANALYTICS-GROWTH MODEL

Starting a new business is easy, growing it is challenging.

It's often hard to figure out what you need to do to increase growth, where to begin, what steps to follow, what data to analyze, what to optimize, and more. The list can go on and on.

Unfortunately, a lot of marketers and business mix growth with conversions, website traffic, app downloads, and other metrics.

Your business grows when it makes more $$$.

The equation is simple.

If your website receives 10K visitors a month but your cash flow is negative and you aren't making a lot of money from these visitors, your business isn't growing.

If your website receives, let's say, 10K visitors. Out of these 10K visitors, 200 add a product to cart, and only 100 pay and checkout. The conversation rate isn't impressive. Though you're getting 10K visitors a month, which is a great achievement.

But you need to see how much you're earning from these 10K visitors.

Visitors don't pay you.

You need to ensure that a decent number of visitors convert and proceed with the purchase. If they add products to cart and don't pay for them, you're still not doing a great job.

The best you can do is take steps to convert visitors into customers. This transition from a visitor to a customer is defined by sales funnel. Optimizing each stage of the funnel and understanding what makes visitors leave your website (leakages), will eventually help you increase sales.

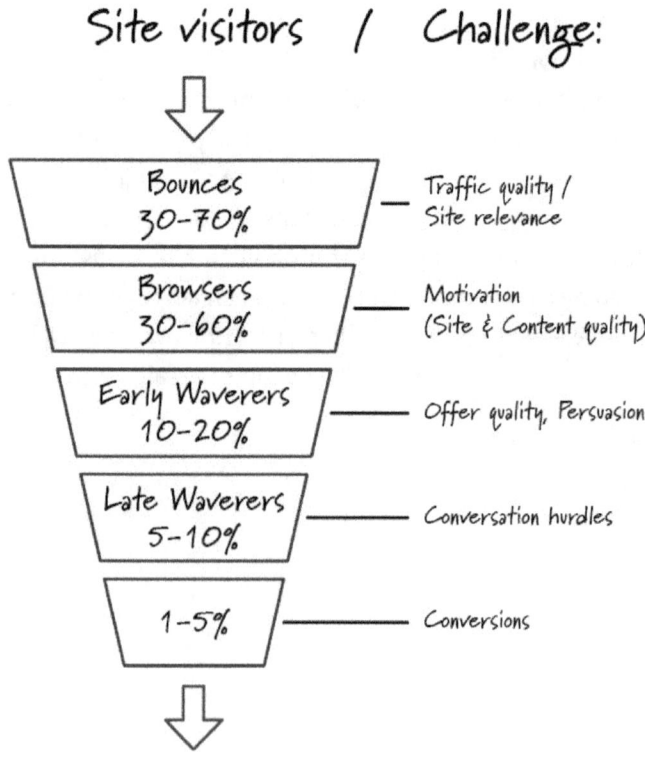

At the end of the day, the only thing that matters is: *How many visitors completed an action that your business thinks to be highly valuable.*

We already defined it as the North Star Metric. Having NSM doesn't mean you can grow your business. You need a complete model with an actionable plan to take your business from zero to all up.

Growth needs to be data-driven and should be powered by analytics. As this is the only way to make growth sustainable. You can do all the guesswork but it won't work in the long-term.

Conversion techniques based on data should be your first and only choice. Here is a 6-step growth formula that you can apply to your business:

1. Define objectives
2. Define critical events
3. Define the North Star Metric
4. Track and measure
5. Analyze
6. Tweak and repeat

Let's visit each of these steps in detail.

Step #1: Define Objectives

It all begins with defining clear objectives for business growth. You need to clearly define what type of growth you intend to drive with analytics and how your business defines growth. Having objectives for your growth plan makes everything streamlined and it gets easier to track progress.

The easiest approach to creating growth objectives for your business is to derive them from business strategy and KPI. You don't have to create growth objectives that don't help you achieve overall business goals or ones that contradict with KPIs. The purpose of using analytics is to help your business (departments and teams) to achieve their goals.

You need to use the SMART technique to create objectives.

This means the objective has to be Specific, Measurable, Achievable, Relevant, and Time-based.

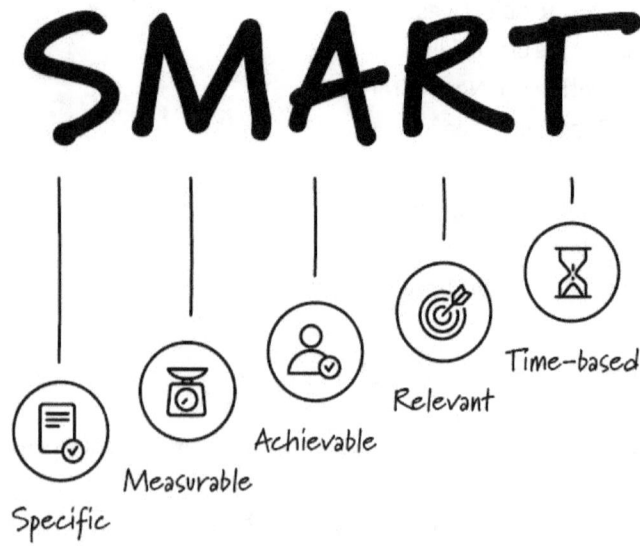

The most important feature of your objective is its relevance to business strategy and KPIs. A standalone growth objective will ruin your business. Your workforce will get confused as to what objective they need to follow for success. Your teams will lose focus and departments will move in different directions.

Here are a few additional tips and techniques that you should focus on when creating growth objectives for your business:

1. The objectives need to be consistent with the business strategy, values, and mission. Ask your management if your growth objective is relevant to values and mission and will it eventually help you achieve annual business goals.

2. The objective should be easy-to-read and easy-to-understand. The language in which you write your objectives should be extremely reader-friendly.

3. Keep objectives concise and to-the-point. Remove fluff. Remove complicated sentences. There shouldn't be any ambiguities in your objectives.

4. Share objectives with your team and departments. Every individual employee in your organization should have a clear understanding of growth objectives and he/she should know what is expected of him.

5. The objective shouldn't be too easy. It needs to be challenging enough. If your employees can achieve it easily, it's not challenging. You need to tweak it and make it more challenging next year.

Here is an example of a few SMART growth objectives that will give you a good idea of how to create one (or more) for your business:

Increase revenue by 15% in one year

Acquire 50K customers in one year

Increase sales by 30% in 9 months

What happens next when you create and select growth objective? You need to share it with your employees. Different departments and managers will create their goals to achieve this objective. You can't achieve objectives in isolation so you have to share it with every individual in your company. That's how it will be achieved.

Step #2: Define Critical Events

The second step is to identify critical events in your sales funnel that will help you achieve your objectives. Any event that holds a significant value for your business is considered valuable.

For instance, adding a product to cart, filling a form, adding a payment method, sharing a blog post, subscribing to your newsletter, etc. are all valuable events.

After you have identified all the critical events throughout the customer lifecycle journey, the next step is to understand what triggers users to complete this event. That is, why a user converts and take the desired action on your website or app.

You can identify and understand these events via your analytics tool. It will show you what users do and why they do it. With your analytics tool, you have to define the user events that you want to track.

You need to identify a single event to begin with that's directly linked to the objective you created in the first step. Choose an event that's most relevant and is extremely high value.

For instance, if your objective is to *acquire 50K customers in one year*, the most relevant event is app download or sign up or when a user enters payment details. What event ensures customer acquisition is determined by data. You have to refer to your analytics tool to see what the most appropriate event is.

In marketing, these events are called *conversions* and to increase or decrease conversions, you need to identify variables that are associated with the conversion. A change in a variable will either positively or negatively impact conversions.

It is important that you choose the right variable that's actually responsible for the conversion. This is why you have to create hypotheses and test multiple variables to finally identify what works and what doesn't.

Let's take an example.

Let's assume Airbnb released a new website to see if it will improve conversion rate. They decided to compare the *Total Number of Nights Booked* before and after the website rollout. Results show that the number of nights booked after the new website skyrocketed.

Clearly the new website has been successful.

Not really.

What if the website was released, say, in October – right before the holidays when everyone is looking for places to stay?

Suddenly it all becomes less relevant.

It is, therefore, extremely important to identify and measure right events, variables, and metrics for sustainable business growth.

Step #3: Define the North Star Metric

The NSM has been discussed in detail in the previous chapter, it is strongly recommended to read everything about NSM before proceeding.

The North Star Metric, coined by GrowthHackers CEO Sean Ellis, is the one metric that captures the core of your business's success, and the one that shows your business is headed in the right direction.

Why you need a single metric?

Because it makes the *Big Goal* of your business clear. It eliminates confusion and your teams know what their big goal is.

North Star Metric helps your business move in the right direction, it bolsters sustainable growth, it supports one goal, it is simple, and it supports team alignment.

All the leading companies have North Star Metrics that help them stay focused and move in the right direction. For instance:

- Uber: Total number of rides completed
- Medium: Total reading time
- Facebook: Total active users each month
- Yours: _____

Your North Star Metric should align with the core value of your business. Hila Qu, the VP of Growth at Acorns, did an outstanding job of defining how to find your North Star Metric:

- The metric should be reflective of your core value.
- The metric should be related to user engagement and activity level.
- The metric should encapsulate all forms of growth.
- The metric should be simple to understand and actionable.

The metric doesn't have to be perfect. You can change it if you feel like you got it wrong or is no longer applicable. But defining a metric that represents the core value is what will get you moving forward.

For example, Quora's core value is "*Facilitate the sharing of knowledge in the world.*" The metric that means the most to them is the number of questions answered. They could have had a metric such as "*Number of questions asked*" or "*Number of users on site per day*" but that wouldn't be in line with their core value.

So how is this NSM relevant to the business objectives, critical event, and growth?

You need to identify NSM that's relevant to the objective you identified in Step #1 and it should be relevant to the critical event. If you can do so, your business will move in the right direction without any issues.

Refer back to the customer acquisition growth objective example. Your objective is to acquire 50K new customers in one year for your business. This objective is perfect for growth because when you'll have 50K customers, your business will generate revenue automatically.

You have already identified the critical event that's most relevant to customer acquisition. This event needs to be derived from your analytics tool, it shouldn't be an arbitrary event. Let's assume, data shows that a user who enters is payment detail is 92% more likely to stay with your business for at least one year. Now you know the event, it is payment detail information or in other words, trial-to-paid conversion.

In order to track this event, you need to identify a metric (NSM). It could be trial-to-paid conversion or it could be free signups depending on what's more relevant to your business's success. This is again where data will help you.

Let's assume, data shows that 75% of free app users become paid customers. This number isn't bad at all. You need to consider several other factors before choosing the NSM. You could either go for app downloads, free signups, or trial-to-paid conversion. Ask yourself what's more relevant?

Everything about the NSM is great except it has to be found.

It's not one of those metrics that are explicitly (or even implicitly) visible or one that you can calculate with a mathematical formula.

Every business has its own unique NSM metric. You have to find your business's NSM to move forward.

Before finding your business's most essential metric that will put your business on the right track, there are a few critical things that should be considered.

1. The NSM has to be **customer-driven**.
2. It should be a **single** metric.
3. It should be **quantifiable**.
4. It should be linked to sustainable **growth**.

With this in mind, let's see how you can find the NSM for your business.

1. Data Analysis

The first step towards finding the NSM is to analyze all (or at least most of) the existing data that you have. This includes buyer personas, KPIs, customer behavioral analysis, buying patterns, retention rate, acquisition cost, etc.

Try finding answers to the following questions:

What are the most critical success metrics and KPIs for your business?

What makes customers satisfied?

What is the core problem that your product solves?

How do success and failure look like from the business's perspective?

How does the customer journey look like?

The answers to these (and any other related) questions will reveal information that will help you move in the right direction. What's important is that you define customer and business success clearly. Customer success isn't always what your business considers to be a _success_.

For instance, your customers might consider signing up for the _Free Trial_ as a success while your business might define success in the terms of the number of paid customers who switch to a premium plan after the expiration of the free trial.

There should be a clear distinction between how your customers define success and what you consider to be a success.

Data analysis will provide you with answers to several questions related to customers, the value they get from your product, and what they expect from your product. This will give you a basic idea of what your NSM will look like.

2. Predictive Values

An important approach that can help you identify NSM for your business is positive predictive value. When you initially identify metrics for NSM, you have to compare them to figure out what's most relevant NSM that truly defines success.

This is where you can use positive and negative predictive values to figure out what metric is most suitable for your business. You need to identify user actions that predict success. The idea is to group users based on actions they have taken and then analyze each group's behavior after completion of the action.

Does a specific group engage more after action completion than other groups?

What actions your most engaged users take and the path to the engagement status they follow. Because once you know the actions that highly engaged users take, you can stick with that metric for growth.

In reality, there isn't any set actions or behavior that you can identify by looking at the data. Depending on your product, sales funnel, onboarding sequence, and business strategy, there could be several actions that a user should take to achieve success or there could be just a few actions.

Ideally, you'll come up with multiple user segments with varied actions and the journey they follow to achieve success. This is where you need to compare different groups using predictive values. Positive and negative predictive values help you identify the best-performing segment that meets or exceeds your criterion.

So let's suppose, you have identified two different user groups with high engagement that you think are most essential for your business and you have identified paths to success for each group:
   1.Log in to the app for 7 consecutive days
   2.Invite 3 friends to use the app

The problem?

You don't know the most appropriate set of actions that users should take. And that's where you have to use predictive values. Here is how to calculate them:

Positive Predictive Value = True Positives / (True Positives + False Positives)
Negative Predictive Value = True Negatives / (True Negatives + False Negatives)

A high percentage of positive predictive value is desirable which means that your assumption is correct that if users complete a specific action, they're most likely to stick around.

Let's take a real-life example.

Uber analyzed the actions its most engaged users take and data revealed the following actions:

1.Booking 5 trips in 7 days
2.Inviting 3 friends in 7 days
3.Spending $100 in 7 days

The data shows that all the three groups are highly engaged but it doesn't show you what's the most engaged group with highest engagement and retention level after a few months (let's say 3 months). This is something that can be found with the help of predictive values.

Uber found negative and positive predictive values for the three groups based on 3-month retention. The group with the highest positive predictive value for 3-month retention is the one that Uber should choose.

Let's assume that the following are the positive and negative predictive values:

1.Booking 5 trips in 7 days ==> Positive predictive value = 99%, Negative predictive value = 96%

2.Inviting 3 friends in 7 days ==> Positive predictive value = 97%, Negative predictive value = 45%

3.Spending $100 in 7 days ==> Positive predictive value = 95%, Negative predictive value = 51%

This shows that booking 5 trips in 7 days has the highest positive predictive value for 3 months and having fewer than 5 trips in 7 days has strong negative predictive value for 3 months. This is clearly the best user action that defines engagement and retention.

Now this might seem a lot of number crunching and it might seem difficult to calculate predictive values. Here is the good news: There are analytics tools out there that will do it for you such as Air360. The predictive values are calculated automatically based on analytics and your job gets a whole lot easier because you know what exactly you're supposed to do.

3. Identify Core Product Value

The North Star Metric is focused on the value that loyal customers drive from your product. This is what you should identify when you have all the data.

It is essential to merge both customer success and business success. If your loyal customers drive value from your product that isn't your product's core feature (or success), there is something not right that has to be fixed first.

However, this rarely happens.

Consider Facebook. Their NSM is defined in terms of active users and that's actually what majority of the Facebook users consider to be of value (they like being signed in to their

Facebook account so they can interact with friends and explore their News Feed). However, not all Facebook users sign in to their accounts daily.

You have to further analyze different critical metrics based on your product, niche, and industry. For instance, if you have a SaaS company, the metrics that you should look for are monthly active users, monthly active users' growth percentage, app stickiness, retention, subscriptions, and subscription upgrades.

It's also a good idea to conduct interviews from customer success managers to get better insights into what customers consider to be of value when using your product.

4. Explore Customer Journey

Customer journey analysis will reveal a lot of information about your business's NSM. Identify sales funnel and see what journey users follow to convert from customers to loyal customers and what makes them stick with your brand.

Every business has a sales funnel, even if you didn't create one. There is always a customer journey path that all customers follow.

For instance, here is how Facebook's customer journey looks like:

1. Visit Facebook.
2. Create a new account.
3. Update information, add a profile picture, and invite friends.
4. Explore Facebook.
5. Visit again to check the News Feed.

The purpose of the customer journey is to let customers get

to the point where they can drive value from the product. Exploring the customer journey will let you know the most appropriate metric that describes core value.

Note: Customer lifecycle journey (sales funnel) is covered in Chapter #6.

5. Test and Tweak

Finding the NSM isn't a simple task. You have to deal with multiple metrics and it will get challenging to pick one metric that's most relevant. It is never easy, especially for large businesses.

You need to test the core value you identified. It might not be the right core value for your business.

Now there isn't any straightforward approach to testing and figuring out if you have identified the right NSM.

The customer should get the value from your product. There are multiple ways to identify if it is actually happening. Surveys and customer interviews are best approaches to see if they're actually getting the value they deserve.

Data analysis will reveal a lot of information.

Refer back to the Facebook example. If customers aren't logging in to their Facebook accounts, it means they're not getting the value they're supposed to get.

There could be several reasons as to why customers aren't becoming active users and that's the tricky part.

This calls for extensive testing and tweaking. After you have identified a metric that you think is the NSM, it has to be tested to make sure it actually is the right NSM for your business.

Don't hesitate to tweak or even entirely change the NSM. Don't haste.

6. Finalize the NSM

Constant monitoring, testing, and tweaking will help you finalize the North Star Metric for your business that will lead to sustainable growth.

The idea is to make sure that the NSM captures value delivered to the customers.

Incorporate core value into customer journey (aka sales funnel) so customers can easily get to the point where they can achieve success with your product and engage further.

You need to help customers get value from your product so every customer makes it to the NSM.

Think customer onboarding which is aimed to help customers achieve first success with the product. When a customer achieves first success with your product, the engagement increases significantly.

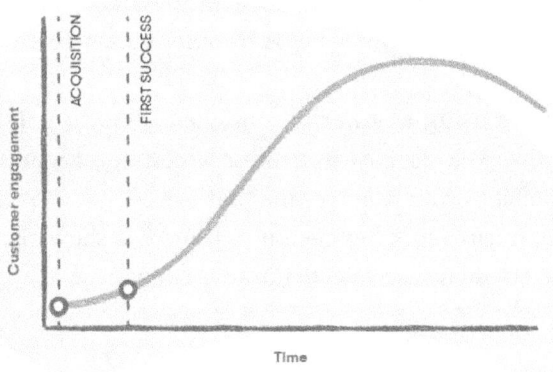

This is what exactly you should do to help customers reach the point where they can get value from your product.

Once you have successfully identified the NSM, the next step is to communicate it and let everyone know about it. Ensure that all the teams work on achieving the NSM either directly or indirectly.

Step #4: Track and Measure

Now that everything is set up and ready, it's time to start tracking the NSM for business growth.

You need to implement an appropriate analytics tool that will track the NSM (refer to the previous chapter to identify an appropriate analytics tool). Measuring and tracking help you figure out how changes affect your ability to improve your business and the North Star Metric.

Your analytics tool should track all the events and user behavior. The more data it collects, the better it is. It should track everything ranging from clicks to mouse movement to buttons clicked to landing pages to actions taken to events and beyond.

If you're using a powerful tool like Air360, it will handle everything. You just have to create an account, get your tracking code, add it to your website, and that's it.

It will track events, segment users, and will show insights as to what steps you can take to improve conversions.

Step #5: Analyze

Most businesses would stop the growth process after they have implemented their analytics tool. Once it starts tracking and measuring the NSM, they will relax.

And that's one of the biggest mistakes that any business could make. Not analyzing the analytics tool is a mistake that could cost you a lot.

Tracking and measuring aren't enough rather you have to analyze data that your tool generates. The tool you're using is only responsible for tracking the events and the metrics for which it is designed. It does its job. It doesn't tell you if you're tracking the right metric that will lead to growth.

This is something that you have to do. How you use its reports and data is all up to you.

What if you identified the wrong NSM for your business? And let me tell you something, a lot of businesses identify and track the wrong NSM that doesn't lead them anywhere.

Your tool will continue tracking the NSM even if it isn't right for your business and even if it doesn't help your business with growth. You have to interfere and analyze what's happening and if things are moving in the right direction.

I have to admit that analyzing your analytics tool critically and making sense of the data is challenging. It's not easy to figure out if you're tracking the right metrics and events. There isn't any alert button.

For instance, Google Analytics shows you a lot of metrics ranging from bounce rate and unique visitors. How you make sense of the data is up to you. It doesn't tell you if you have to monitor the bounce rate to analyze UX. It just tracks and reports.

Same is the case with any other analytics tool. It reports −

and that's it.

This is why it's essential to analyze what you're tracking. And if you figure out that your NSM isn't correct or if your objectives are misleading and aren't aligned to KPIs, you need to revise them. Don't hesitate to adjust and tweak your NSM.

An important aspect of the analysis is to keep track of the progress. Are you moving in the right direction? Are departments and teams achieving goals? Are you achieving monthly goals?

It is better to constantly analyze the progress instead of waiting for the end-year. You need to generate reports from the analytics tool to keep track of the progress and fix issues as they're found. Don't wait. Don't waste time. Be consistent.

Step #6: Tweak and Repeat

After you see positive results in the analysis and you have realized that the objectives set in the first step are now achieved, don't stop there. Move ahead and repeat the process next year and every year.

What most of the businesses do is that they stick with the same objective (after they achieve significant growth with it) for the next few years. For instance, if the objective was to acquire 50K new customers, they will stick with the same objective next year and so on.

They do it because they see results.

Don't do it. You need to tweak the objectives and make it more challenging next year. If you have achieved your objective successfully, it means your team has the potential. If you'll set somewhat similar objective next year, it will make your team less productive so in order to make it challenging and to grow your business more, set higher objectives.

For instance, if you successfully acquired 50K customers in 10 months (instead of a year), you should set 90K customer acquisition next year (at least).

Your analytics tool will provide you with a lot of information on how much your team is capable of and what percentage of new customers were acquired daily, weekly, and monthly. This data will make objective-setting easier. If, for instance, data analytics show that you acquired 5K customers a month, this means your business has the capacity to acquire 60K customers a year easily. You need to set objectives accordingly.

If, on the other hand, you failed to achieve the objective, you still need to tweak it. Refer to analytics and data to see what went wrong. Was it negligence or was your team didn't have the potential to achieve the objectives? Your analytics tool plays a significant role in the tweaking phase.

You don't have to tweak the objective rather you need to tweak anything and everything that will help your business grow next year. It could include resource allocation, budgeting, new recruits, critical events, CRO techniques, metric revision, analytics tool update, and more.

The idea is to find a winning growth formula for your business and improve it every year. Don't stop when you find the formula for growth, you need to improve it. Make it better.

You never know the limit unless you try it.

It's just like conversions rate. There is always a chance to improve unless you achieve 100% conversion rate. Anything less than 100% means there is a chance to improve. In the case of growth, there isn't any limit. You can have unlimited growth. All you have to do is continue improving and doing it over and over again.

8

CHAPTER #6: ULTIMATE BUSINESS GROWTH TECHNIQUES

You have learned everything about growing your business with analytics and you know the 6-step growth formula to take your business to the next best level. You need to master a few advanced business growth techniques that will guide you in the right direction.

Here is the thing: Having the right analytics tool for your business won't help if you don't know what to measure. You need to understand the basics of how your website works.

You need to understand the sales funnel because it provides you with the most actionable data. It shows you why your business isn't growing as expected.

Understanding Sales Funnel

A sales funnel is a journey that a customer goes through when making a purchase on your website. Refer back to AARRR framework which is a sales funnel for SaaS companies.

Here is a sales funnel (or customer lifecycle journey) that's commonly used by all types of business:

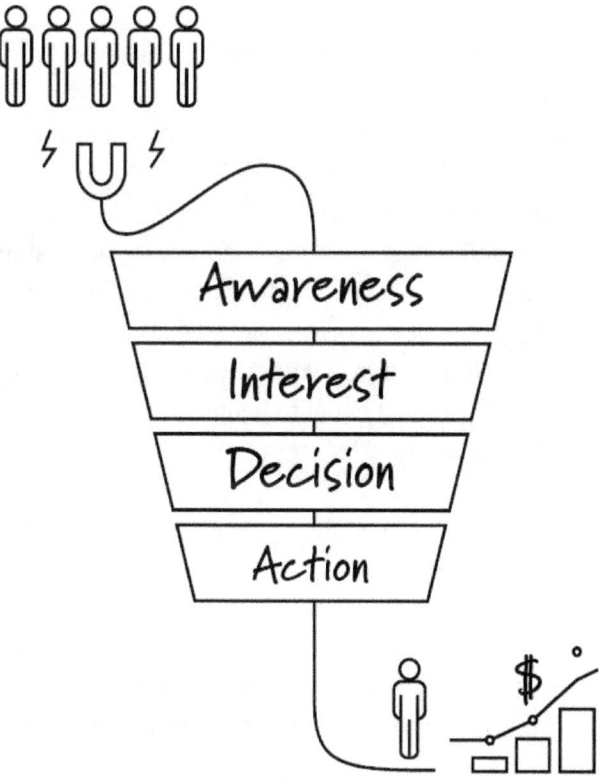

A sales funnel could take any form and could have any stages but, generally, it has four main stages:

1. Awareness
2. Interest
3. Decision
4. Action

Every business has a sales funnel. Even if you haven't created one, you still have it.

Because visitors always go through multiple stages to convert into customers. Whatever steps they follow to complete their journey, it's your sales funnel.

It is best to define customer lifecycle stages to understand it, track it, and increase conversions – and grow your business.

The core purpose of each stage is to push as many people to the next stage. You need to make sure that people entering the funnel should be almost equal to people leaving your funnel. You need to reduce funnel leakages.

How?

To understand why people leave your company without becoming a customer.

Let's assume, 1000 people visit your website (Stage 1). This is where they have entered the funnel. Only 100 move to the next stage where they convert to prospects and show interest in your product. And only 10 become customers in the last stage.

Iamge4

This means your funnel leaked 900 people in Stage 1 and 90 in Stage 2. These are the people who didn't convert. You can improve this by optimizing your funnel for conversions.

How'd you feel if all the 1000 people who enter the website become customers? There are no leakages at all.

It will be amazing, right?

The sales will skyrocket.

This can be achieved by reducing leakages which is known as conversion optimization. You need to improve the conversion rate across all the stages of the sales funnel.

This is where analytics help you.

The true value of analytics is in the ability to look at detailed dimensions based on highly specific data – everything from the browser visitors' use to the size of their screen. While many data collection tools make it theoretically possible to find this information, most lack the user-friendliness necessary to both:

1. Figure out how to find the information you need.
2. Feel confident that you have found that information correctly.

Even if you were able to, say, find an answer to a question within your Google Analytics data, the amount of work that would go into finding that answer would be substantial, and chances are you would not feel confident that it was completed correctly.

It's why most businesses utilize user-analytics tools, which are built around the user and their needs rather than around a database of complicated data to wade through.

Air360, for example, is a tool specifically designed to be immensely intuitive with no need to hire a data expert. You can figure out how to find the answers you need.

And of course, beyond the tool, it is important to think of your website or app as a funnel and not a hierarchy. This is what will help you find actionable insights that will grow your conversions and revenue.

Now that you know what a sales funnel is and how it works, let's cover the stages of a conventional sales funnel in detail.

1. Awareness Stage

This is the top of the funnel when you make the first contact with a potential customer. The customer becomes aware of your brand. This first awareness interaction could be driven by a post on Facebook, a Google search query, or a brand mention a forum.

The moment a potential customer gets to know your brand for the very first time, he enters awareness stage and from that moment onwards, he stays in the awareness stage for all the future interactions unless he starts taking interest in your brand.

For instance, Sam found your brand the first time when his friend tagged in him one of your Facebook posts. The post was informational so the prospect didn't know what you're offering. He didn't like your page either. (First interaction)

A few days later, the same prospect saw your ad in Google search while running a query. He clicked and landed on your website. He browsed your website for a few minutes and then left without buying. (Second interaction)

Next day, he saw your product recommendation on Instagram by an influencer. He visited your website again, followed you on Instagram and liked your Facebook page. (Third interaction).

And so on.

Sam had three interactions with your brand but he didn't buy yet neither he show any interest in any of your products. He is still in the awareness stage.

A potential customer could spend any number of days in the awareness stage. Some of them will leave your brand altogether after a few interactions (called leakage) and others might purchase on their very first visit. The time an individual spends in the awareness stage (or any other stage in the funnel) is not known but you can track it over time with decent analytics and/or tracking tool.

Once you start tracking visitors, you get to know them better. You can calculate the average time spent in the awareness stage. You can then reduce the time and leakages.

The awareness stage is all about your ideal customers getting to know your brand and products.

2. Interest Stage

Not all potential customers will move to the interest stage. Only those who will find a mutual fit and will like your products will move to the interest stage. Others will leave forever.

No matter how hard you try, you can't convince everyone to move down the funnel. There will always be leakages. You need to minimize leaks but don't let leaks let you and your team down. These leaks are faced by all the big brands like Google and Amazon. You can find negative reviews about Google, Amazon, PayPal, and pretty much any big brand name on the internet.

A lot of people don't like these big brands.

So it is natural.

Interest stage is when ideal customers start doing research and they start comparing your products with alternates. Not all potential customers will compare products, some of them will buy right away and others will spend a lot of time reading reviews etc.

A lot of people will enter your funnel at the interest stage. Not all of them follow the exact same stages. For instance, someone who read your product review and a comparison post on an authority blog will start his journey from interest stage.

Refer back to Sam.

Sam subscribed to your newsletter after having three interactions with your brand. He explored your website and is now looking to solve his problem.

Sam has entered the interest stage. He knows what products you're offering but he is not sure if he should buy. He is still in the research phase.

3. Decision Stage

This is the stage when the prospect is ready to buy and is considering your product as well. The decision stage is when the prospect is deciding what to buy. He might buy from you or from a competitor.

When a prospect is in the decision-making stage, he is actively involved in product comparisons. He is looking for a solution to his problem. If your product is valuable enough, he will consider yours too.

Refer back to Sam.

Sam has visited your pricing page and has explored the product features page. He has read product comparison articles on your blog and is now looking for a product that will solve his problem. He is considering multiple products including yours.

Again, the decision stage isn't a must. A good chunk of potential customers jumps from interest to purchase skipping the decision stage. It depends on how you interact with them in the interest stage (more on this coming next). If you manage to show them that your product is best in the game, they will make their mind and will go with your product without having to spend days in the decision stage.

How many times have you purchased a product on Amazon

instantly without a second thought? This is what happens with a lot of people who enter your sales funnel. They will just buy and move on.

Nevertheless, a lot of people spend a few good days in deciding what to buy especially if it is a high-end expensive product.

4. Action Stage

This is the bottom of the funnel where prospects convert to customers by buying your product. The action refers to purchase which means people decide to buy your product.

Sam, after spending a few good days in the decision stage, finally purchases your product and becomes your customer.

This is the final stage in the funnel but the interaction doesn't end here. You don't want to have a single sale per customer, or do you?

What you should do is build a relationship with your customers and encourage them to buy more. This is why a lot of businesses use an additional stage called Retention stage. This is the stage where you retain your customers, engage with them, and convert them to repeat customers.

The idea is to increase the Average Lifetime Value of your customers because it is easier to sell to an existing customer than to a new customer.

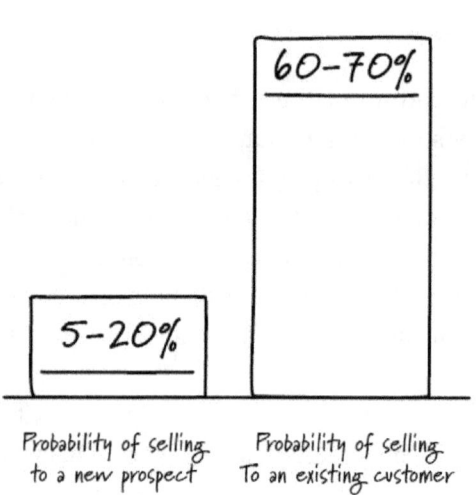

Probability of selling to a new prospect

Probability of selling To an existing customer

Refer back to Sam.

Sam has purchased one product and now you have sent him a discount coupon to purchase another product from your store. Sam avails the discount and becomes a repeat customer.

And it continues...

Now that you know how sales funnel and its stages work,

let's proceed to growth strategies for each stage. In the sections below, we will cover growth techniques that you can incorporate at each stage for exponential growth.

Let's get started.

1. Growth Techniques for Awareness Stage

The awareness stage is all about making it easier for your ideal customers to know you. It's about showing them who you're. Your audience doesn't know you at this stage, they don't know much about your products, and they don't know anything about your brand at all.

So you have to provide information about your brand and should show your audience who you're. And that's it.

You don't have to tell about your products, services, and offers at this stage – it won't work. Rather you need to tell about your brand, your brand story, what you do, why you sell what you sell, and deliver valuable content.

Selling or pre-selling at this stage is suicidal. It will turn visitors away. Don't do it. Never do it.

Here is what you should do instead in the awareness stage to attract your ideal customers and to avoid leaks at this stage.

Know Your Audience

The first logical thing you have to do at the awareness stage is to understand visitors. Even if you have created buyer personas, you have done a lot of market research, and you have spent a lot of money on audience research, you still need to incorporate tracking and analytics tool to understand visitors.

Why?

To verify if you're receiving the right type of traffic.

If you're receiving the right people (as expected), no further action is needed. This will verify your buyer personas. You're targeting the right people.

However, if visitors aren't converting and despite getting a lot of traffic, it isn't working, there seems to be something wrong. Analytics will reveal patterns and behavioral analytics will show if you're receiving right people on your website.

In this case, you'll have to tweak your buyer personas. Seek help from your analytics tool. Get to know the characteristics and behavior of the visitors.

Air360, for instance, lets you analyze the behavior of each visitor. You can see what action a visitor took on your website. You can segment visitors automatically for better targeting.

The data will let you know your audience better in the awareness stage, what will happen next...

Publish Valuable Content

... You can provide them with what they're most interested in.

This is the sole purpose of awareness stage – to dig deep, use analytics, and publish valuable content that your audience will interact to.

The biggest challenge is creating and publishing the right content in the awareness stage. Since the purpose of the awareness stage is to make visitors aware of your brand, here are a few types of content you should create:

1. EBooks
2. Whitepapers
3. How-to guides
4. Reports

5. Educational content

The content should deliver value, it shouldn't pre-sell. You need to create high-value content that will make readers fell in love with your brand and content. You need to prove yourself as an authority. It is a great idea to create 10x content. Here is an overview of how to create 10x content:

10X CONTENT
CHARACTERISTICS

Solves a problem/question through comprehensive, accurate, exceptional information and resources

Is different in scope and detail from other work on similar topics

Loads quickly and has great UI across any device and browser

Creates an emotional response (awe, surprise, joy, anticipation, admiration)

Delivers great user experience with the use of fonts, visuals, patterns, structure...

Provides content that is a combination of high quality, trustworthy, useful and interesting

When you start publishing high quality content, the next step is identifying what type of content readers love interacting with so you can create more of that content type specifically. This is where your analytics tool plays a significant role. It will show you how much time visitors spend at the top, middle, and bottom of the post, where they click, etc.

For instance, if analytics show that a lot of people like how-to guides, you need to create more how-to guides. If visitors don't like whitepapers, you need to stop creating them.

Let analytics guide your awareness stage content.

Refrain From Selling

If there is one thing that you should NEVER do in the awareness stage, it's selling.

Why?

Someone who is reading a how-to guide on your blog isn't interested in buying rather he is only interested in understanding how to solve a specific problem.

If you'll use CTAs in your high-quality content, you'll ruin conversions. This is not how it works. You don't have to ruin awareness stage content by pitching your products. You need to do it at the right stage (decision stage).

The rule is simple: Decide the purpose of each content piece you create. Is it for awareness stage, is it to develop interest, or is it to generate leads? When the content purpose is clear, you'll create content that will attract the right people and leaks throughout the funnel will reduce.

2. Growth Techniques for Interest Stage

Interest or consideration stage is where you try developing an interest in your brand and content without getting too salesy. You need to develop interest in your products too.

The prospects at this stage are interested in solving their problem and are looking for solutions. They may or may not know about your product so your job is to show them your solution. You need to make them realize you offer a solution to their problem.

The first thing you should do to develop prospect interest is to start tracking them. This is done by a tracking tool which means you need to track what they do on your website and off your website. Those who move from the awareness stage to the interest stage have visited your website a few times (at least once).

If you have a tracking tool enabled, you'll know what they're interested in and how they're moving ahead with your brand. You can show them the content they can't refuse. This is the best way to develop their interest in your products.

Content Type

The content type for interest and consideration stage is more about your brand and your products. You still have to create valuable content but you have to show them your products too. You have to tell them that you also offer a solution to their problem.

The content you have to create at this stage include:
1. Whitepapers
2. Solution comparisons
3. Expert guides
4. Videos
5. Podcasts

The flow of the content for this stage should be something like this:
1. Create educational and informative content

2. Show solutions to the reader's problems
3. Pitch your product as a solution to the problem

You have to keep this content type different than awareness stage content. Don't mix them both. Don't create a single piece for all funnel stages.

If you publish 2 pieces of content per week (including text, videos, podcasts, infographics, etc.) you can create one piece for awareness stage specifically and the other piece for interest stage prospects.

Your analytics and funnel tool guide you in terms of what type of content you need to create. If, for instance, your business objective is to acquire new customers, you'll have to create a lot of awareness stage content to attract new prospects.

Use data to guide your growth strategy for the interest stage.

3. Growth Techniques for Decision Stage

This is the stage where you can do all the selling without any hesitation. You need to show prospects that your product stands out from the rest. Since prospects are in the decision-making phase so you have to pitch your product hard here.

You don't have to create hype. You don't need to set very high expectations. Just pitch your product, describe its benefits, and tell prospects how it will solve their problem. That's it.

The best content at this stage of the funnel includes:

1. Product comparisons
2. Free trials
3. Product reviews
4. Case studies
5. Tradeshows

6. Case studies

Not all content types perform equally well so you have to figure out what's working for your brand. There are several things that you have to take care of at this stage:

1. Focus on the benefits of your product instead of features.
2. Don't set very high expectations of the prospects. Describe the true picture of your product.
3. Highlight the unique selling proposition of your product. The prospects compare different solutions to their problems and they will choose yours if it is better than all the other available solutions. Tell them how your product is different yet better.
4. Publish a lot of video content as it works best at this stage. It's better to show instead of telling.

4. Growth Techniques for Action Stage

Prospects finally convert, take action, and become customers. This is the bottom of the funnel where the real magic happens. Those who make it to the bottom of the funnel are the ones who are more likely to buy because they have spent a lot of time with your brand (and have moved from the top to the bottom of the funnel).

Your job is to make conversion easier, simple, and obvious.

Not all the prospects know what action they have to take after they have read a great comparison article on your blog. Even if they're impressed with your product and ready to buy, if there aren't any clear instructions on what they should do to buy your product, they might leave.

This is where you have to use a Call-To-Action (CTA). A CTA tells the prospects what action they have to take in order to buy your product. Or, it tells them what to do next.

A CTA could be a button, text, or in any other form. CTAs should be used throughout your blog and on your website. Needless to say, the content targeting bottom of the funnel should have multiple CTAs to ensure those who have made their mind can grab your product without a hitch.

Single Grain uses three powerful CTAs above the fold on its blog and website. Why? Because the guys at Single Grain know they have to guide prospects to conversion.

Here are a few techniques to creating compelling CTAs that will drive conversions:

1. Keep CTAs descriptive. Instead of using '*Click Here*', switch to '*Click here to get 7-days free trial*'.
2. Make CTA action-oriented.
3. Describe the benefit in CTA. Tell readers why they should click it and what they will receive in return.
4. Add at least one CTA above the fold.
5. Use different types of CTAs (text as well as buttons).
6. Make CTA prominent. It should stand out from the crowd.
7. Add white space around CTA to avoid clutter. White space improves readability.
8. Test, test, and test your CTA.

CTAs aren't just needed on your website but you have to incorporate them everywhere on the internet including social networks, videos, PDF, slides, and more. Whenever and wherever you publish (or syndicate) content, make sure it isn't without at least one CTA.

Whenever you add a CTA, it has to be tested. A wrong CTA

at the wrong place won't work. A right CTA at the wrong place won't work either. How do you find what's the right CTA type and what's the most appropriate location?

By testing.

This is where you have to use a CRO tool like VWO. You have to create multiple CTAs and run A/B tests to see which one works better. Hook this data from CRO tool to your analytics tool to spot differences in traffic sources and to identify how traffic from different sources respond to CTAs.

Data can make things easier so as the right tools.

5. Growth Techniques for Retention Stage

Retention is an additional stage in the sales funnel that is often used by several businesses especially SaaS companies. After a prospect has successfully taken the action and converted to a customer, you have to retain him.

Retaining isn't just enough rather you have to persuade your customers to buy again. You need to convert them into repeat customers. Repeat customers are critical to any business because they spend 33% more than new customers.

Repeat customers

spend **33%** more

than new customers

Laura Lake

Why?

Because they have been through your business for quite some time. They know you. They have spent time in the sales funnel and have tried your product at least once. Besides, repeat customers become your loyal customers. They stick with your brand and might bring in new customers (through referral).

New customers, on the other hand, have to move through the sales funnel and they need time to trust your brand and product.

If your sales funnel ends at the action stage, you're not optimizing it. In fact, you're losing money. You don't want this to happen, right? This is against the rules of growth. If you really want to grow your business, you need to convert every customer into a repeat customer.

And it's not that hard.

According to Paul Farris, a repeat customer has a 60-70% chance of converting. This means you don't have to put a lot of effort into persuading your existing customers to buy again. Here are a few techniques that you can incorporate to convert customers into repeat customers:

1. Engage, engage, and engage. Don't leave your customers alone after they have reached the bottom of the funnel. Interact with them via email, social network, and other channels.
2. Use customer data and profiles to pitch them products they're most likely to buy. You have to integrate data from CRM and analytics tool to identify buying behavior.
3. A customer loyalty program is your best bet to convert customers into repeat customers.
4. Send emails regularly to customers regarding new products, discounts, etc. You have to show them that you care.
5. Provide exceptional customer services. This is one of the best ways to impress customers and encourage them to do more business with your brand.

Not all customers buy again. Some of them might leave your company after a single purchase due to any number of reasons. You need to have a retention strategy to retain those customers. Don't let customers go easily.

You should reduce churn by predicting customer behavior. This is something that Air360 does exceptionally well. It uses AI to predict churn and you get to know customers who are most likely to churn. You can get in touch with them, offer them assistance, or at least ask why they're leaving.

If nothing else works, get feedback to improve flaws in your business/product that are making customers churn.

The bottom of the funnel only ends where you want it to end. Theoretically, it should never end. Customers should move from one stage to another and must stick with your brand forever. That's how you'll grow your business exponentially.

9

CHAPTER #7: FUTURE OF ANALYTICS

You know how to use data from your analytics tool to drive growth. That's awesome.

What if I tell you that there are tools that you can use to go a step further...

Yes, there are tools that will do analysis, decision-making, and everything for you on your behalf. The tool will identify opportunities, test different variations, and will implement best-performing variation.

Sounds interesting, right?

It's not a joke rather it's a reality.

The data analytics tool generates data. You need to make sense of it. You have to use data to see what it actually means. You have to find links within your data to make sense of it.

For instance:

- 75% of Netflix users choose their next film based on the recommendation algorithm.
- 35% of Amazon's total sales are from their recommendation algorithm.

· 50% of LinkedIn engagement comes from the "*Jobs You May Be Interested In*" feature.

All the leading businesses use powerful algorithms that use heaps of data to identify patterns. The decisions by the algorithm have an immediate financial impact.

Netflix's recommendation system is believed to reduce drop-off rate dramatically with some estimates pointing at over 1 billion per year. This is achieved by using data to keep viewers engaged.

They get all this data through analytics.

But it's not manual data entry that helps them create these features, nor is it manual data mining that uncovers these opportunities. These connections are made using artificial intelligence (AI).

I started working with artificial intelligence as a software engineer all the way back in 2001 before AI was considered *COOL*. Back long before it was mainstream, AI was seen as something from science fiction. While we're still decades away from robots that enslave the human race the progress we've made in AI is remarkable.

Computers are way better than humans ever could be at analyzing large amounts of data in minimal time.

Aggregated data is not useful enough for analysis. Behavioral data is where the valuable information is and it is perhaps the most tedious task that can be completed by humans.

If humans have to monitor all the data such as visitors with different devices, browsers, screen sizes, languages, referral sources, feature usages, etc., and then have to analyze what content they read and where their journey began, it will take forever.

You can't do it manually, let's admit it.

So when I started Air360, the mission was not to create another user analytics platform that could collect and chart data. It was to create a platform that would help humans save time and money to see a massive increase in their ROTI – Return of Time Invested.

The newer and modern analytics tools use Artificial Intelligence to do the work that human beings are not equipped to do. It gives instant real-time results so you can use the intelligence you are equipped to do to figure out the next steps.

For example, our analytics software is capable of figuring out who is "About to Churn" – which users, based on their behavioral data, are most likely to quit and why.

Companies like Netflix have used this specific data to figure out how to best address the needs of the users that are most likely to leave based on their usage patterns. They created a segment that allows them to easily identify the customers at risk, gain insights into why they became at risk, and monitor how changes to their algorithm affect it over time.

Businesses of all sizes can take advantage of these insights to reduce customer loss, improve sales, and so much more. All the data is delivered to you automatically through insights via the AI.

Artificial Intelligence and Analytics

Artificial Intelligence (AI) and Machine Learning (ML) are the two most famous buzzwords of the current century. Both AI and ML are impacting all types of sectors including businesses and of course analytics.

AI is defined as:

"The science and engineering of making computers behave in ways that, until recently, we thought required human intelligence."

This is what exactly we do at Air360. It uses science and engineering to make predictions that help you in decision-making and analytics. When there is heaps of data that needs to be analyzed (in case of big data), you need powerful algorithms and help from AI.

According to the Capgemini Digital Transformation Institute, as much as 79% of organizations that implement AI successfully generate new insights and improve analysis. There isn't any doubt that both analytics and AI make a superb couple and when used right, you can kill the competition.

When AI is coupled with analytics, your analytics get better and smarter. Here is an example of how the couple works together.

You have an app and you're using an analytics tool that tracks user behavior. It can identify patterns based on the most common actions that users who are about to churn take. It will track the last few actions taken by churned users and will let you know (in the future) whenever a user is about to churn.

Another more general example could be:

Your analytics tool is designed to send a notification when sales reduce to a significant level. Whenever your ecommerce store generates sales less than the threshold, you'll get the notification. A normal analytics tool will continue sending notifications without monitoring trends. An AI enabled analytics tool, on the other hand, won't send notifications when the sales decline due to an event. If sales decline every Monday because it's the first working day of the week and your store doesn't receive a lot of traffic on Monday, the AI-powered analytics tool will identify the trend and won't send you notifications on Monday but it will send notifications on other days when sales decline due to any other reason.

In today's time, it isn't a nice idea to use an analytics tool that doesn't come with AI or ML. Not only that such a tool will be able to predict the future but it has the potential to deal with massive data.

Advances in the Internet of Things (IoT) provides businesses with more data that they can manage (and handle). In such a time, you can't go without AI-powered analytics tool. You definitely need them now.

Where to Go From Here

The road ahead is not easy. Analytics, AI, IoT, and ML will prove to be game changers in the near future. Clearly, there isn't any way forward without an analytics tool.

The more data you'll have, the better it is.

The more data you analyze, the better.

And you have to be quick at data analysis. The quicker, the better.

What you need to do is start using a powerful analytics tool, track users across multiple devices and channels, focus on personalization, prepare for augmented reality, and use AI and ML.

There isn't any alternative.

Sooner or later, you have to do it to stay in the business. If you need to grow your business, you have to do it NOW.

If you're already using an analytics tool and you think it is doing a great job, that's great.

If you're using an analytics tool but aren't satisfied with its performance, change it before it gets too late.

If you're not using any analytics tool, grab one today.

10

CHAPTER #8: THE LAST WORDS

You have to realize that analytics is 50% tool and 50% people and culture. The way how you use your analytics tool is more important than the tool itself.

For example, a single analytics tool is used by hundreds and thousands of businesses. You and your competitor might be using the same analytics tools but you don't perform equally well in terms of data analytics.

Why?

Because it's not just the tool that has to work – your team, organizational culture, and organizational structure play their role too. It's more about developing a data culture in your business where each employee breathes data.

For instance, ManoMano redefined its data culture around four principles: Autonomy, accessibility, agility, and agnosticism. They didn't change the analytics tool, it remained the same rather they redefined their culture.

And it worked.

So while you're busy finding the right analytics tool, don't forget to tweak your organization's culture and your workforce's attitude towards data. It's equally important, if not more important than having a top-notch analytics tool.

The progress we've made in the analytics and AI world is exciting yet encouraging Analytics can help websites and apps to increase revenue and growth. It also helps you create a better and more engaging product by using all the data that your tool collects and analyzes.

However, businesses are still struggling. Almost 60% of companies are not doing even the bare minimum of analytics necessary to find problems. Almost none of them segment users based on user data and many do not have any analytics software at all.

But analytics is more powerful than ever.

It's easier than ever.

It's more useful than ever.

There is no reason to ignore the value that analytics can have for your business and it's up to you as you're the decision maker.

Make it happen.

Best,

Flo

www.ingramcontent.com/pod-product-compliance
Lightning Source LLC
Chambersburg PA
CBHW072139170526
45158CB00004BA/1443